KNOW YOUR BIBLE

FOR TEEN GUYS

KNOW YOUR BIBLE

FOR TEEN GUYS

BARBOUR
PUBLISHING

ISBN 979-8-89151-214-6

Devotional entries written by A.L. Rogers.

Published by Barbour Publishing, Inc., 1810 Barbour Drive, Uhrichsville, Ohio 44683, www.barbourbooks.com

Our mission is to inspire the world with the life-changing message of the Bible.

Member of the Evangelical Christian Publishers Association

Printed in China.

IT HELPS EVERYTHING TO KNOW YOUR BIBLE

Barbour Publishing's *Know Your Bible* paperback has helped millions of people to understand God's Word better. Now, for the first time, that little book's easy-to-understand, clarifying content has been packaged especially for teen guys.

Inside this book, you'll find quick, concise details on scripture. . .the most important facts plus the context you need to grasp how everything fits together. Read on for

- Genesis-to-Revelation book summaries, featuring particulars on the author and date of writing, an "In Ten Words or Less" description of each book, a longer "Details, Please" summary, one or more key verses, and a list of "Unique and Unusual" features of each book
- a 365-day Bible reading plan, including thumbnail sketches of each passage to provide a helpful overview of scripture's story
- and 20 challenging, encouraging devotions introducing you to key men of God's Word

This book features the fresh-yet-familiar text of the Barbour Simplified King James Version Bible, along with a handful of quotations from the popular New International Version.

It helps everything to know your Bible. And *Know Your Bible for Teen Guys* helps you do just that!

GENESIS

AUTHOR

Not stated but traditionally attributed to Moses.

DATE

Moses lived around the 1400s BC, but the events of Genesis date to the very beginning of time.

IN TEN WORDS OR LESS

God creates the world and chooses a special people.

DETAILS, PLEASE

The Bible's first book never explains God; it simply assumes His existence: "In the beginning God. . ." (1:1). Chapters 1 and 2 describe how God created the universe and everything in it simply by speaking: "God said. . .and it was so" (1:9, 11, 14–15). Humans, however, received special handling, as "God formed man from the dust of the ground and breathed into his nostrils the breath of life" (2:7); woman was crafted from a rib of man. Those first two people, Adam and Eve, lived in perfection but ruined paradise by disobeying God at the urging of a "subtle" (or crafty, 3:1) serpent. Sin throws humans into a moral freefall as the world's first child—Cain—murders his brother Abel. People become so bad that God decides to flood the entire planet, saving only the righteous Noah, his family, and an ark (boat) full of animals. After the earth repopulates, God chooses a man named Abram as patriarch of a specially blessed people, later called "Israel" after an alternative name of Abram's grandson Jacob. Genesis ends with Jacob's son Joseph, by a miraculous chain of events, ruling in Egypt—setting up the events of the following book of Exodus.

QUOTABLE

- God said, "Let there be light," and there was light. (1:3)
- The Lord said to Cain, "Where is Abel your brother?" And he said, "I do not know. Am I my brother's keeper?" (4:9)

- But Noah found grace in the eyes of the Lord. (6:8)
- He [Abram] believed in the Lord, and He counted it to him for righteousness. (15:6)

UNIQUE AND UNUSUAL

Genesis quickly introduces the concept of one God in multiple persons, a concept later called the Trinity: "God said, 'Let Us make man in Our image, according to Our likeness'" (1:26). Also early on, God gives a hint of Jesus' future suffering and victory when He curses the serpent for deceiving Eve: "I will put enmity between you and the woman, and between your offspring and her offspring; He shall bruise your head, and you shall bruise His heel" (3:15).

SO WHAT?

Genesis answers the great question "Where did I come from?" Knowing the answer can give us meaning in a world that's otherwise hard to figure out.

DAY 1

GENESIS 1–3

God creates the beautiful world and everything in it. Humanity soon falls into sin as Adam and Eve disobey God's one rule.

DAY 2

GENESIS 4:1–7:9

Sin spreads quickly, to the point that God decides to cleanse the entire world with a flood.

DAY 3

GENESIS 7:10–10:32

God instructs Noah, the world's only righteous man, to build a large boat to save himself, his family, and at least two of each kind of animal from the coming flood.

DAY 4

GENESIS 11–14

God chooses a childless man named Abram to begin a "great nation"

DAY 5

GENESIS 15–18

God changes Abram's name to Abraham ("father of a multitude"), promising that his ninety-year-old wife, Sarah, will give birth to a son.

DAY 6

GENESIS 19–21

Hundred-year-old Abraham and ninety-year-old Sarah become parents of Isaac, whose name means "laughter."

DAY 7

GENESIS 22–24

God commands Abraham to sacrifice Isaac, then stops him at the last moment, saying, "you have not withheld your son, your only son, from Me."

DAY 8

GENESIS 25–27

Abraham dies and God repeats His promise to Abraham through Isaac and Isaac's second-born son, Jacob.

DAY 9

GENESIS 28–29

God confirms His promise of blessing to Jacob, who falls in love with a cousin, Rachel. But Jacob is tricked by her father into marrying her sister, Leah, too.

DAY 10

GENESIS 30–31

Jacob's two wives and two of their servants give birth to eleven sons, who will become leaders of the "tribes of Israel."

DAY 11

GENESIS 32–34

Jacob meets a mysterious "man" who wrestles him; the man changes Jacob's name to Israel, "for as a prince, you have power with God and with men and have prevailed."

DAY 12

GENESIS 35–36

Jacob's favored wife, Rachel, gives birth to his twelfth son, Benjamin, then dies; Isaac also dies, at age 180.

DAY 13

GENESIS 37–39

Jacob's favorite son, Joseph, is sold into slavery by his jealous older brothers. He goes through terrible hardship in Egypt by holding fast to God, who gives him success.

DAY 14

GENESIS 40–41

Using his God-given ability to interpret dreams, Joseph predicts a coming famine and tells Pharaoh how to prepare. Joseph is made second in command of all Egypt.

DAY 15

GENESIS 42–43

Joseph's brothers, also facing famine in Canaan, arrive in Egypt to buy grain. Without realizing it, they stand before the man they had sold into slavery.

DAY 16

GENESIS 44–45

Joseph tests his brothers before finally telling them who he is. They are terrified, but he speaks kindly to them.

DAY 17

GENESIS 46–48

Jacob, who had long believed Joseph was dead, arrives in Egypt for a joyful reunion. Jacob's family is allowed to settle in Egypt.

DAY 18

GENESIS 49–50

The dying Jacob speaks a blessing over each of his sons, and dies at age 147. Jacob says his son Judah will produce a ruler—and today we know that means Jesus!

KNOW YOUR BIBLE *MEN*

ADAM

GOD'S REPRESENTATIVE

So God created man in His own image, in the image of God
He created him; male and female He created them.
GENESIS 1:27

†

Professional athletes rarely handle their own contract negotiations. They review their offers with a representative called an agent. The agent does the hard work of figuring out the contract, which requires detailed knowledge of legal documents and the player's market value. Most athletes are primarily focused on their game, so the agent represents the athlete's interests. He makes sure any contract the player signs is honest and fair.

The Genesis story reveals that God made human beings as His representatives on earth. But we're not reviewing contracts—our job is much more important. People were set apart from everything else God made to be caretakers, representing God's glory and honor as we rule over creation (Genesis 1:26; Psalm 8:4–6). Being made in the image of God is both a blessing and a responsibility.

God gave Adam specific jobs that filled his life with purpose. As you grow in your faith, you'll sense God's calling to be a caretaker. . .over a job, a family, a ministry, or something else. Whatever it is, following God faithfully will fill your life with purpose too.

You are made in His image. You are one of His agents. Whatever God gives you to care for, represent His goodness to the world.

Heavenly Father, thank You for making
me in Your image. You are good, creative,
and wise. Please grow these qualities in me
and help me to care well for others.

EXODUS

AUTHOR

Not stated but traditionally attributed to Moses. In Exodus 34:27 God tells Moses, "Write these words," and Jesus, in Mark 12:26, quotes from Exodus as "the book of Moses."

DATE

Approximately the mid-1400s BC.

IN TEN WORDS OR LESS

God delivers His people, the Israelites, from slavery in Egypt.

DETAILS, PLEASE

The Israelites prosper in Egypt, having settled there at the invitation of Abraham's great-grandson Joseph, who entered the country as a slave and rose to second in command. When Joseph dies, a new pharaoh sees the burgeoning family as a threat—and makes the people his slaves. God hears the Israelites' groaning, remembering "His covenant with Abraham, with Isaac, and with Jacob" (2:24) and raising up Moses as their deliverer. God speaks through a burning bush, and Moses reluctantly agrees to demand the Israelites' release from Pharaoh. To break Pharaoh's will, God sends ten plagues on Egypt, ending with the death of every firstborn child—except those of the Israelites. They put sacrificial blood on their doorposts, causing the Lord to "pass over" (12:13) their homes. Pharaoh finally allows the Israelites to leave the country (the "Exodus"), and God parts the Red Sea for the people, who are being pursued by Egyptian soldiers. At Mount Sinai, God delivers the Ten Commandments, rules for worship, and laws to change the family into a nation. When Moses delays on the mountain, the people begin worshipping a golden calf, bringing a plague upon themselves. Moses returns to restore order, and Exodus ends with the people continuing their journey to the "promised land" of Canaan, following God's "pillar of the cloud" by day and "pillar of fire" by night.

QUOTABLE

- God said to Moses, "I AM THAT I AM." And He said, "You shall say this to the children of Israel, 'I AM has sent me to you.'" (3:14)
- "This is what the LORD says: 'Let My people go.'" (8:1)
- "When I see the blood, I will pass over you." (12:13)
- You shall have no other gods before Me. (20:3)

UNIQUE AND UNUSUAL

God told the Israelites to celebrate the "Passover" with a special meal of bread made without yeast (12:14–15). Three thousand years later, Jewish people still commemorate the event.

SO WHAT?

The story of redemption is on clear display in Exodus as God rescues His people from their slavery in Egypt. In the same way, Jesus breaks our bonds of sin (Hebrews 2:14–15).

DAY 19

EXODUS 1–3

After Joseph dies, Egypt sees the Israelites as a threat and makes them slaves. God calls Moses to be the deliverer of His people.

DAY 20

EXODUS 4–6

Moses, with the help of his brother, Aaron, confronts Pharaoh with God's message: "Let My people go."

DAY 21

EXODUS 7–9

God sends horrible plagues on the people and land of Egypt. But Pharaoh's heart is hardened and he refuses to let the Israelites leave.

DAY 22

EXODUS 10–12

In the last of ten plagues, God kills the firstborn of every family without the blood of a sacrificial lamb on its doorposts. God will "pass over" the obedient Israelites' homes.

DAY 23

EXODUS 13–15

On their way out of Egypt, the Israelites are pursued by Pharaoh's army. God parts the Red Sea to provide an escape route for His people, then destroys the Egyptian soldiers.

DAY 24

EXODUS 16–18

On their way through the wilderness, the Israelites complain of hunger and thirst. God provides miraculous food ("manna") and water from a rock.

DAY 25

EXODUS 19–20

God calls Moses up Mount Sinai, giving him laws for the nation of Israel. God's rules are highlighted by the Ten Commandments.

DAY 26

EXODUS 21–23

God gives Moses more laws for Israel, dealing with personal relationships, private property, and national religious events.

DAY 27

EXODUS 24–27

God establishes three feasts, calls His people to obedience, and tells Moses how to build the tabernacle, a large, movable tent that will serve as Israel's worship center.

DAY 28

EXODUS 28–29

God explains the job and requirements for Israel's priests, under the leadership of Aaron and his family.

DAY 29

EXODUS 30–31

God tells His people how to worship and supplies gifted craftspeople for all He has called the Israelites to make for the tabernacle. He reminds His people to rest on the Sabbath day so that the workers could be refreshed.

DAY 30

EXODUS 32–33

When Moses returns from Mount Sinai, he finds the people worshipping a calf idol they had demanded during his absence. Moses prays for the people, and God decides not to destroy them completely.

DAY 31

EXODUS 34–35

As the Israelites move toward the Promised Land, the Lord demands that they remain separate from the godless people already living there.

DAY 32

EXODUS 36–38

Two gifted artists oversee construction of the tabernacle—Israel's portable worship tent—using materials given by the people as offerings.

DAY 33

EXODUS 39–40

God's glory, like a cloud, fills the finished tabernacle. The cloud will lead the Israelites on their journey to the Promised Land.

LEVITICUS

AUTHOR

Not stated but traditionally attributed to Moses.

DATE

Approximately the mid-1400s BC.

IN TEN WORDS OR LESS

A holy God explains how to worship Him.

DETAILS, PLEASE

Leviticus, meaning "about the Levites," describes how that family line should lead the Israelites in worship. Ceremonial laws—as opposed to the moral laws of Exodus—describe offerings to God, dietary restrictions, and purification rites. Special holy days—including the Sabbath and Passover—are commanded. The family of Aaron, Moses' brother, is ordained as Israel's formal priesthood. Leviticus lists several blessings for obedience and many more punishments for disobedience.

QUOTABLE

- "You shall be holy, for I [God] am holy." (11:44)
- "The life of the flesh is in the blood. . .it is the blood that makes an atonement for the soul." (17:11)

UNIQUE AND UNUSUAL

Leviticus' blood sacrifices are contrasted with Jesus' death on the cross: "Who does not need, as those high priests, to offer up daily sacrifices. . .for He did this once when He offered up Himself" (Hebrews 7:27).

SO WHAT?

Though we don't live under the rules of Leviticus, we still serve a holy God—and should treat Him as such.

DAY 34

LEVITICUS 1–4

Rules for the Levites, Israel's priests and helpers, are laid out. Various offerings to God—the burnt, peace, and sin offerings—are explained.

DAY 35

LEVITICUS 5–7

Trespass offerings, covering a wide range of sinful behaviors, are explained.

DAY 36

LEVITICUS 8–10

Israel's priests are set apart and begin their duties. Aaron's sons Nadab and Abihu lose their lives for breaking the laws on offerings to God.

DAY 37

LEVITICUS 11–12

God describes the types of food the Israelites may eat ("clean") and that must be avoided ("unclean") and the laws concerning the birth of a child and the mother's purification.

DAY 38

LEVITICUS 13:1–14:32

God lays out rules for dealing with "leprosy," a term describing various skin diseases.

DAY 39

LEVITICUS 14:33–15:33

God describes how people and houses can be cleansed, physically and ceremonially, from skin diseases.

DAY 40

LEVITICUS 16–17

Rules are provided for Israel's annual Day of Atonement. Atonement—paying for sin—is only accomplished by the shedding of innocent blood.

DAY 41

LEVITICUS 18–20

The Israelites are commanded to be pure in heart and body, to avoid false worship, and to "be holy to" God.

DAY 42

LEVITICUS 21–23

Priests are commanded to maintain a high level of purity, staying away from anything that would lead to sin.

DAY 43

LEVITICUS 24–25

Various rules demand payback for crimes, the death penalty for blaspheming God, and an agricultural "sabbath" every seventh year, when the land is allowed to rest.

DAY 44

LEVITICUS 26–27

God promises blessings for obedience and punishment for disobedience. And He predicts a time when Israel will be scattered from the Promised Land.

KNOW YOUR BIBLE *MEN*

NOAH

FAITHFUL UNDER PRESSURE

By faith Noah, being warned by God of things not yet seen, moved with fear, prepared an ark to the saving of his house.
HEBREWS 11:7

Everyone wants to fit in. You can feel it—at school, on the team, even at church, people are secretly afraid of being left out. No one wants to sit alone in the lunchroom. No one wants to be singled out as weird. When our fear of being left out becomes overwhelming, we're tempted to give in to peer pressure. We might compromise who we are in order to be accepted.

The pressure to fit in must have been enormous for Noah. Humankind had been overcome with wickedness (Genesis 6:5, 11). Yet Noah—and his family—remained faithful. Then God asked Noah to build an enormous boat called an "ark." It was a massive project that likely took years to complete. Imagine how Noah's neighbors must have ridiculed him: *Why are you building a giant, worthless boat on dry land?* But Noah obeyed God (Genesis 6:22).

The people around Noah made God angry enough to destroy them. Your peers will not upset God to that point. But they may pressure you to destroy yourself. Others may push you to make choices you know are wrong, even just "little compromises" that will erode your identity as a follower of Jesus.

Stand fast against that peer pressure. Have faith, as Noah did, in God's ways. Even if that means you're sometimes left out, a life spent walking with God is far better than anything anyone else could offer.

Lord God, help me to stand fast against peer pressure. Thank You for always giving me a place to belong. Help me to share Your goodness with others.

NUMBERS

AUTHOR

Not stated but traditionally attributed to Moses.

DATE

Approximately 1400 BC.

IN TEN WORDS OR LESS

Faithless Israelites wander forty years in the wilderness of Sinai.

DETAILS, PLEASE

Numbers begins with a census—hence the book's name. Fourteen months after the Israelites escape Egypt, they number 603,550 men, not including the Levites. This mass of people, the newly formed nation of Israel, begins a march of approximately two hundred miles to the "promised land" of Canaan—a journey that will take decades to complete. The delay is God's punishment of the people, who complain about food and water, rebel against Moses, and hesitate to enter Canaan because of powerful people already living there. God decrees that this entire generation (except Joshua and Caleb) will die in the wilderness, leaving the Promised Land to a new generation of more obedient Israelites.

QUOTABLE

- "The Lord is longsuffering and of great mercy, forgiving iniquity and transgression." (14:18)

UNIQUE AND UNUSUAL

Even Moses misses out on the Promised Land, punishment for disobeying God by striking, rather than speaking to, a rock from which water would miraculously appear (20:1–13).

SO WHAT?

God hates sin and punishes it. We can be thankful that Jesus took that punishment for us.

DAY 45

NUMBERS 1–2

Fourteen months after leaving Egypt, in the wilderness of Sinai, God tells Moses to count the Israelites. (That's where the name Numbers comes from.)

DAY 46

NUMBERS 3–4

God claims the tribe of Levi as His tabernacle servants, with Aaron's family as priests and other family lines managing the worship center itself.

DAY 47

NUMBERS 5–6

God commands His people to be pure and holy, and outlines a special level of separation, the Nazarite vow.

DAY 48

NUMBERS 7

The tabernacle is dedicated in a twelve-day celebration highlighted by the giving of gifts by the individual tribes.

DAY 49

NUMBERS 8–10

The people of Israel hold their first Passover dinner after leaving Egypt. Then the cloud of God's presence leads them out of the Sinai wilderness.

DAY 50

NUMBERS 11–12

The people quickly complain about God's manna and bring judgment on themselves; even Moses' siblings Aaron and Miriam grumble against his leadership.

DAY 51

NUMBERS 13–14

Moses sends twelve spies to check out the Promised Land. Ten frighten the people with reports of giants. God says only the faithful spies Joshua and Caleb will enter Canaan.

DAY 52

NUMBERS 15–16

Doomed to forty years of wandering in the wilderness, the Israelites are still taught how to worship the Lord. The rebellion of Korah the Levite leads to thousands of deaths.

DAY 53

NUMBERS 17–19

Aaron's staff—his walking stick—miraculously blossoms and produces almonds, proving that his family is God's choice for priests.

DAY 54

NUMBERS 20–21

When they lack water, the people rebel. An angry Moses disobeys God and is banned from the Promised Land. The complaining Israelites, punished by poisonous snakes, are healed by looking to a brass serpent on a pole.

DAY 55

NUMBERS 22–24

An enemy king hires a non-Israelite prophet, Balaam, to curse God's people; God turns the tables, causing Balaam to bless them instead.

DAY 56

NUMBERS 25–27

God calls for another census of Israel, numbering the younger people who will enter Canaan after the older generation dies off. Joshua is named as leader after Moses.

DAY 57

NUMBERS 28–30

God tells Moses to remind the people of the various offerings and feasts to be observed once they arrive in Canaan.

DAY 58

NUMBERS 31–32

At God's command, Israel goes to war against Midian. These people had earlier urged God's children to commit sins like idolatry.

DAY 59

NUMBERS 33–34

The Israelites consider their past journey, then prepare to enter the Promised Land, with the leader of each tribe called to help to divide Canaan among the people.

DAY 60

NUMBERS 35–36

Israel's worship leaders, the Levites, do not get their own territory but will spread out through Canaan in forty-eight "cities of refuge."

DEUTERONOMY

AUTHOR

Traditionally attributed to Moses, an idea supported by Deuteronomy 31:9: "Moses wrote this law and delivered it to the priests. . .and to all the elders of Israel." Chapter 34, recording Moses' death, was probably written by his successor, Joshua.

DATE

Approximately 1400 BC.

IN TEN WORDS OR LESS

Moses reminds the Israelites of their history and God's laws.

DETAILS, PLEASE

With a name meaning "second law," Deuteronomy records Moses' final words as the Israelites prepare to enter the Promised Land. Forty years have passed since God handed down His laws on Mount Sinai, and the entire generation that experienced that momentous event, aside from Joshua and Caleb, has died. So Moses reminds the new generation both of God's commands and of their national history as they ready their entry into Canaan. The invasion will occur under Joshua, as Moses will only see the Promised Land from Mount Nebo. "So Moses the servant of the LORD died there. . . . And He [God] buried him in a valley in the land of Moab. . .but no man knows of his burial place to this day" (34:5–6). Moses was 120 years old.

QUOTABLE

- "Hear, O Israel: The LORD our God is one LORD." (6:4)
- "You shall love the LORD your God with all your heart and with all your soul and with all your might." (6:5)
- "The LORD your God is a jealous God among you." (6:15)

UNIQUE AND UNUSUAL

The New Testament quotes from Deuteronomy dozens of times, including three from the story of Jesus' temptation in the wilderness in Matthew 4:1–11. The Lord defeated Satan by restating Deuteronomy 8:3 ("Man shall not live by bread alone, but by every word that proceeds out of the mouth of God"); 6:16 ("You shall not tempt the Lord your God"); and 6:13 ("You shall worship the Lord your God, and Him only shall you serve").

The Ten Commandments, most commonly found in Exodus 20, are restated in full in Deuteronomy 5.

SO WHAT?

Deuteronomy makes clear that God's rules and expectations aren't meant to limit and frustrate us but instead to benefit us: "Therefore hear, O Israel, and be careful to do it, that it may be well with you, and that you may increase mightily as the LORD God of your fathers has promised you, in the land that flows with milk and honey" (6:3).

DAY 61

DEUTERONOMY 1–2

Moses reminds the Israelites of God's promise of Canaan, the people's refusal to enter the land, and their forty-year punishment of wandering in the wilderness.

DAY 62

DEUTERONOMY 3–4

As the new generation of Israelites prepares to enter Canaan, Moses reminds the people what He God already done for them and teaches the people the "statutes and judgments" of God.

DAY 63

DEUTERONOMY 5–7

Moses repeats the Ten Commandments and shares the great rule, "You shall love the LORD your God with all your heart and with all your soul and with all your might."

DAY 64

DEUTERONOMY 8–11

Moses urges the people to honor God by remembering His care for them during their decades in the wilderness.

DAY 65

DEUTERONOMY 12–14

Moses urges the Israelites to worship as God has commanded, and to destroy any hints of false worship and idolatry in Canaan.

DAY 66

DEUTERONOMY 15–17

Moses reminds the people to observe the Passover and other feasts. And he predicts a day when the Israelites will demand a king to rule over them.

DAY 67

DEUTERONOMY 18–20

Moses tells the people that God will one day raise up a prophet like himself—a hint at the life and ministry of Jesus.

DAY 68

DEUTERONOMY 21–23

Moses gives a variety of laws for Israel, including some that set the people apart from other nations—such as never wearing a garment "of wool and linen together."

DAY 69

DEUTERONOMY 24–26

Moses shares even more laws for the Israelites, including the law of "firstfruits"—they must offer God the first produce of the land.

DAY 70

DEUTERONOMY 27–28

Moses tells the people that curses that will come on Israel for disobeying God, but blessings for following His commands.

DAY 71

DEUTERONOMY 29–31

At age 120, Moses announces his coming death. He commands his helper Joshua to "bring the children of Israel into the land."

DAY 72

DEUTERONOMY 32–34

Moses speaks a final blessing over the people, then climbs Mount Pisgah for a glimpse of the Promised Land before he dies. Joshua takes over the leadership of Israel.

KNOW YOUR BIBLE *MEN*

ABRAHAM

PROMISES FROM GOD

"And I will make of you a great nation, and I will bless you and make your name great, and you shall be a blessing."
GENESIS 12:2

†

Has anyone ever broken a promise to you? Have you ever broken a promise you made to someone else? Those things hurt. When people break promises, you lose trust in them. You realize you can't count on them to do what they said they would do.

Abram (later called Abraham) was given the whopper of all promises. God said He would build a new nation out of this man's family. God also promised that this nation, all of Abram's descendants, would someday bless every person on earth (Genesis 12:1–3). What an incredible promise!

At the time the promise was made, though, Abram was childless. His wife couldn't bear children (Genesis 11:29–30). But in faith, he trusted God's promise (Hebrews 11:8–11). The rest of the Old Testament tells the story of this nation, Israel, before Jesus arrived on earth as a baby in Bethlehem. The New Testament then demonstrates that Jesus, an Israelite Himself, is the blessing for all peoples on earth (John 3:16). God kept His promise.

As your relationship with God grows, you'll discover more of His promises in the Bible—like the ones in James 4:8 and Romans 8:1. Memorize those promises and live in faith as Abram did. The Bible reveals that God is and always has been a promise keeper. You can count on Him to do whatever He says He'll do.

Heavenly Father, I thank You for keeping Your promises. Though other people may let me down, You never will. Help me to follow wherever You lead.

JOSHUA

AUTHOR

Traditionally attributed to Joshua himself, except for the final five verses (24:29–33), which describe Joshua's death and legacy.

DATE

Approximately 1375 BC.

IN TEN WORDS OR LESS

The Israelites capture and settle the promised land of Canaan.

DETAILS, PLEASE

With Moses and an entire generation of disobedient Israelites dead, God tells Joshua to lead the people into Canaan, their promised land. In Jericho, the first major obstacle, the prostitute Rahab helps Israelite spies and earns protection from the destruction of the city: God knocks its walls flat as Joshua's army marches outside, blowing trumpets and shouting. Joshua leads a successful military campaign to clear idol-worshipping people—Hittites, Amorites, Canaanites, Perizzites, Hivites, and Jebusites—from the land. At one point, God answers Joshua's prayer to make the sun stand still, allowing more time to complete a battle (10:1–15). Major cities subdued, Joshua divides the land among the twelve tribes of Israel, reminding the people to stay true to the God who led them home: "Now therefore, put away the foreign gods that are among you and incline your hearts to the Lord God of Israel" (24:23).

QUOTABLE

- "Be strong and of good courage. Do not be afraid or be dismayed, for the Lord your God is with you wherever you go." (1:9)
- "One man of you shall chase a thousand, for the Lord your God is He who fights for you, as He has promised you." (23:10)

- "Choose for yourselves this day whom you will serve. . .as for me and my house, we will serve the Lord." (24:15)

UNIQUE AND UNUSUAL

Joshua is one of few major Bible characters who seemed to do everything right—he was a strong leader, completely committed to God, who never fell into recorded sin or disobedience. Only one mistake mars his record: Joshua's experience with the Gibeonites, one of the local groups he should have destroyed. Fearing for their lives, they appeared before Joshua dressed in old clothes, carrying dry, moldy bread, claiming they had come from a faraway land. Joshua and the Israelite leaders "did not ask for counsel from the mouth of the Lord" (9:14) and agreed to a peace treaty. When Joshua learned the truth, he honored his agreement with the Gibeonites—but made them slaves.

SO WHAT?

Joshua shows over and over how God blesses His people. The Promised Land was His gift to them, as were the military victories that He engineered.

DAY 73

JOSHUA 1–2

God encourages Joshua in his new role as leader of Israel; he sends men to spy out the Promised Land at the fortified city of Jericho.

DAY 74

JOSHUA 3–5

To enter the Promised Land, the Israelites cross the Jordan River, miraculously parted by God. Joshua meets "the captain of the LORD's army."

DAY 75

JOSHUA 6–8

Following God's battle plan—march around Jericho and watch its walls collapse—Joshua and the Israelites begin their conquest of Canaan.

DAY 76

JOSHUA 9–10

The people of Gibeon trick the Israelites into letting them live. Joshua honors the promise but makes the Gibeonites servants to Israel.

DAY 77

JOSHUA 11–13

Joshua and the Israelite army defeat thirty-one pagan kings in their fight for Canaan. As he nears the end of his life, Joshua oversees division of the land to the tribes of Israel.

DAY 78

JOSHUA 14–16

Eighty-five-year-old Caleb, the only faithful spy (besides Joshua) sent to the Promised Land decades earlier, is given land as a reward.

DAY 79

JOSHUA 17–19

With the Promised Land largely in their hands, the Israelites set up the tabernacle, their tent of worship, at Shiloh.

DAY 80

JOSHUA 20–22

"Cities of refuge" are set up to protect people who accidentally kill others. Tribes that settled east of the Jordan River build an altar and have to convince the other Israelites that they are truly worshipping God.

DAY 81

JOSHUA 23–24

The dying Joshua speaks a final command to Israel: "Choose for yourselves this day whom you will serve. . . as for me and my house, we will serve the LORD."

JUDGES

AUTHOR

Unknown; some suggest the prophet Samuel.

DATE

Written approximately 1050 BC, covering events that occurred as far back as 1375 BC.

IN TEN WORDS OR LESS

Israel goes through cycles of sin, suffering, and salvation.

DETAILS, PLEASE

After Joshua's death, the Israelites lose momentum in driving pagan people out of the Promised Land. "The children of Benjamin did not drive out the Jebusites who inhabited Jerusalem" (1:21) is a statement characteristic of many tribes, which allow idol worshippers to stay in their midst—with tragic results. "You have not obeyed My voice" God says to His people. "They shall be as thorns in your sides, and their gods shall be a snare to you" (2:2–3). That's exactly what happens, as the Israelites begin a cycle of worshipping idols, suffering punishment by attackers, crying to God for help, and receiving God's aid in the form of a human judge (or "deliverer") who restores order. Lesser-known judges include Othniel, Ehud, Tola, Jair, and Jephthah, while more familiar figures are Deborah, the only female judge, who led a military victory against the Canaanites; Gideon, who tested God's will with a fleece and defeated the armies of Midian; and the amazingly strong Samson, who defeated the Philistines. Samson's great weakness—his love for unsavory women such as Delilah—led to his downfall and death in a Philistine temple.

QUOTABLE

- They abandoned the LORD God of their fathers, who had brought them out of the land of Egypt, and they followed other gods—gods of the people who were all around them. (2:12)

- The LORD raised up judges who delivered them out of the hands of those who plundered them. (2:16)
- The LORD said to Gideon, "The people who are with you are too many for Me to give the Midianites into their hands, lest Israel boast against Me, saying, 'My own hand has saved me!'" (7:2)

UNIQUE AND UNUSUAL

Several judges had unusual families by today's standards: Jair had thirty sons (10:4), Abdon had forty sons (12:14), and Ibzan had thirty sons and thirty daughters (12:9). Jephthah had only one child, a daughter, whom he foolishly vowed to sacrifice to God in exchange for a military victory (11:30–40).

SO WHAT?

The ancient Israelites got into trouble when they "did what was right in [their] own eyes" (17:6; 21:25) rather than what God wanted them to do. Don't make the same mistake yourself!

DAY 82

JUDGES 1-3

Israel fails to drive out all the residents of Canaan, and these godless people become "thorns in [their] sides." God raises up leaders called judges to defeat Israel's enemies.

DAY 83

JUDGES 4-5

Israel's only female judge, the prophet Deborah, leads the army to victory over the enemy general Sisera.

DAY 84

JUDGES 6-8

God calls the fearful Gideon to be a judge; with only three hundred men, he miraculously destroys the "host of Midian."

DAY 85

JUDGES 9

After Gideon dies, one of his many sons wants to become leader. But he is wicked and dies when a woman in a besieged tower drops a millstone on his head.

DAY 86

JUDGES 10–12

The stories of several judges are told, including that of Jephthah, who lost his daughter after making a foolish promise to God.

DAY 87

JUDGES 13–16

The miraculously strong Samson judges Israel, but he is derailed by selfishness. He will die along with thousands of enemy Philistines when he collapses their temple.

DAY 88

JUDGES 17–19

After Samson's death, Israel—without a leader—falls into idolatry and conflict between tribes.

DAY 89

JUDGES 20–21

Conflict in Israel breaks out into civil war. Sadly, in the days without a king, "every man did what was right in his own eyes."

KNOW YOUR BIBLE *MEN*

JACOB AND ESAU

SIBLING RIVALS

And the boys grew, and Esau was a skillful hunter, a man of the field, and Jacob was a plain man, dwelling in tents.
GENESIS 25:27

†

Super Bowl XLVII (47) featured one of the most famous sibling rivalries in professional football. But it wasn't among players—it pitted the coaches against each other! Jim Harbaugh led the San Francisco 49ers. His older brother, John, coached the Baltimore Ravens. Everyone loved talking about the sibling rivalry that year. Only one brother could lead his team to victory. . .who would it be? How would the other brother handle the loss?

The Bible includes many stories of sibling rivalries (for example, Genesis 4:1–16; 37:1–36; Luke 15:11–32). In Genesis 25, we meet Jacob and Esau, the twin boys of Isaac, the son of Abraham. They were part of the family from which God would build the nation of Israel. But despite their important roles in God's plan, they were in conflict almost their entire lives. They even fought each other in their mother's womb (verse 22). Sibling rivalry is common enough, but it's not helpful. Friendly competition can push brothers and sisters to do their best—in Super Bowl XLVII, John Harbaugh and his Ravens won. But an angry rivalry only creates feelings of resentment. That's why God's Word says, "Behold, how good and how pleasant it is for brothers to dwell together in unity!" (Psalm 133:1).

Heavenly Father, please help me to calm down the intensity of the rivalry I feel within my family—in the home or in the church. Help me to find ways to love and support each one and to live in unity.

RUTH

AUTHOR

Not stated; some suggest Samuel.

DATE

Ruth, the great-grandmother of King David (who reigned approximately 1010–970 BC), probably lived around 1100 BC.

IN TEN WORDS OR LESS

Loyal daughter-in-law pictures God's faithfulness, love, and care.

DETAILS, PLEASE

Ruth, a Gentile woman, marries into a Jewish family. When all of the men of the family die, Ruth shows loyalty to her mother-in-law, Naomi, staying with her and scavenging food to keep them alive. As Ruth gleans barley in a field of the wealthy Boaz, he takes an interest in her and orders his workers to watch over her. Naomi recognizes Boaz as her late husband's relative and encourages Ruth to pursue him as a "kinsman redeemer," one who weds a relative's widow to continue a family line. Boaz marries Ruth, starting a prominent family.

QUOTABLE

- "Where you go, I will go, and where you lodge, I will lodge. Your people shall be my people, and your God my God." (1:16)
- "The LORD recompense your work, and a full reward be given you of the LORD God of Israel, under whose wings you have come to trust." (2:12)
- And the women, her neighbors, gave it a name, saying, "There is a son born to Naomi," and they called his name Obed. He is the father of Jesse, the father of David. (4:17)

UNIQUE AND UNUSUAL

Ruth, from the pagan land of Moab, married a Jewish man and became the great-grandmother of Israel's greatest king, David—and an ancestor of Jesus Christ.

SO WHAT?

We can trust God to provide what we need, when we need it—and to work out our lives in ways that are better than we ever imagined.

DAY 90

RUTH 1–4

A Moabite woman, widow of an Israelite, commits to her mother-in-law and God. Ruth will become the great-grandmother of King David.

1 SAMUEL

AUTHOR

Not stated. Samuel himself was likely involved, though some of the history of 1 Samuel occurs after the prophet's death.

DATE

Approximately 1100–1000 BC.

IN TEN WORDS OR LESS

Israel's twelve tribes unite under a king.

DETAILS, PLEASE

An infertile woman, Hannah, begs God for a son, promising to return him to the Lord's service. Samuel is born and soon sent to the temple to serve under the aging priest, Eli. Upon Eli's death, Samuel serves as judge, or deliverer, of Israel, subduing the nation's fearsome enemy, the Philistines. As Samuel ages, Israel's tribal leaders reject his sinful sons and ask for a king. Samuel warns that a king will tax the people and force them into service, but they insist and God tells Samuel to anoint the notably tall and handsome Saul as Israel's first ruler. King Saul starts well but begins making poor choices—and when he offers a sacrifice to God, a job reserved for priests, Samuel tells Saul that he will be replaced. Saul's successor will be a shepherd named David, who with God's help kills a giant Philistine warrior named Goliath and becomes Israel's hero. The jealous king seeks to kill David, who runs for his life. David rejects opportunities to kill Saul himself, saying, "I would not stretch out my hand against the LORD's anointed" (26:23). At the end of 1 Samuel, Saul dies battling the Philistines, making way for David to become king.

QUOTABLE

- The LORD said to Samuel, "Listen to the voice of the people. . .they have not rejected you, but they have rejected Me, that I should not reign over them." (8:7)

- "Behold, to obey is better than sacrifice and to listen than the fat of rams." (15:22)
- Then David said to the Philistine, "You come to me with a sword and with a spear and with a shield. But I come to you in the name of the LORD of hosts, the God of the armies of Israel, whom you have defied." (17:45)

UNIQUE AND UNUSUAL

The future King Saul is a donkey herder (9:5) who tries to hide from his own coronation (10:21–22). As king, Saul breaks his own law by asking a medium to call up the spirit of the dead Samuel (chapter 28).

SO WHAT?

Selfish choices—such as the Israelites' request for a king and Saul's decision to offer a sacrifice he had no business making—can have heavy, even tragic, consequences.

DAY 91

1 SAMUEL 1-3

Hannah, a woman who can't have children, prays for a son. God answers with the birth of Samuel, who will become the prophet and priest of Israel.

DAY 92

1 SAMUEL 4-6

When he learns that his two sons have died in battle against the Philistines, after the ark of the covenant is captured, Israel's priest, Eli, falls over and dies.

DAY 93

1 SAMUEL 7–9

Samuel prays Israel to victory over the Philistines. Many years later, his evil sons cause the people to demand a king. God tells Samuel to choose Saul.

DAY 94

1 SAMUEL 10–12

Saul is anointed as king, and he begins with an impressive military victory over the Ammonites.

DAY 95

1 SAMUEL 13–14

Saul foolishly tries to do the priests' job, making a burnt offering while waiting for Samuel. Samuel says God will replace Saul with "a man after His own heart."

DAY 96

1 SAMUEL 15–16

Saul disobeys God's command to completely destroy the Amalekites. God sends Samuel to a shepherd boy named David who will become the next king.

DAY 97

1 SAMUEL 17–18

David gains the love of the nation of Israel—and the envy of Saul—by defeating the Philistine giant Goliath with his sling and a stone.

DAY 98

1 SAMUEL 19–20

Saul tries to kill David, who is protected by God and by Saul's son Jonathan, next in line for the throne but David's best friend.

DAY 99

1 SAMUEL 21–23

David runs from Saul, gathers a group of about four hundred fighting men, and hides in the wilderness.

DAY 100

1 SAMUEL 24–25

Given an opportunity to kill Saul, David declines, calling him "the LORD's anointed." Samuel dies. David marries Abigail, widow of the foolish Nabal.

DAY 101

1 SAMUEL 26–28

David again spares Saul's life, then hides among the enemy Philistines. Saul visits a witch to ask for the dead Samuel's guidance and learns he will soon die.

DAY 102

1 SAMUEL 29–31

David becomes friendly with an enemy commander. But when the Philistines get ready to fight Israel, regular soldiers complain. David is forced to leave the Philistines, so he is not present when Saul is killed.

2 SAMUEL

AUTHOR

Unknown but not Samuel—since the events of the book take place after his death. Some suggest Abiathar the priest (15:35).

DATE

Approximately 1010–970 BC, the reign of King David.

IN TEN WORDS OR LESS

David becomes Israel's greatest king—but with major flaws.

DETAILS, PLEASE

When King Saul dies, David is made king by the southern Jewish tribe of Judah. Seven years later, after the death of Saul's son Ish-bosheth, king of the northern tribes, David becomes ruler of all Israel. Capturing Jerusalem from the Jebusites, David creates a new capital for his unified nation, and God promises David, "your house and your kingdom shall be established forever" (7:16). Military victories make Israel strong, but when David stays home from battle one spring, he commits adultery with a beautiful neighbor, Bathsheba. Then he has her husband—one of his soldiers—murdered. The prophet Nathan confronts David with a story of a rich man who steals a poor man's sheep. David is furious until Nathan announces, "You are the man!" (12:7). Chastened, David repents and God forgives his sins—but their consequences will affect David powerfully. The baby conceived in the tryst dies, and David's family begins to splinter apart. One of David's sons, Amnon, rapes his half sister, and a second son, Absalom—full brother to the violated girl—kills Amnon in revenge. Absalom then conspires to steal the kingdom from David, causing his father to flee for his life. When Absalom dies in battle with David's men, David grieves so deeply that he offends his soldiers. Ultimately, David returns to Jerusalem to reassert his kingship. He also raises another son born to Bathsheba—Solomon.

QUOTABLE

- How the mighty have fallen in the midst of the battle!(1:25)
- "Who am I, O Lord God? And what is my house that You have brought me here?" (7:18)
- "O my son Absalom, my son, my son Absalom! I wish to God I had died instead of you, O Absalom, my son, my son!" (18:33)

UNIQUE AND UNUSUAL

David's nephew killed a Philistine "of great stature who had six fingers on every hand, and six toes on every foot" (21:20). David's top soldier, Adino, once killed 800 men single-handedly (23:8).

SO WHAT?

King David's story highlights the vital importance of the choices we make. Who would have guessed that such a great man could fall into such terrible sin?

DAY 103

2 SAMUEL 1–2

David learns of Saul's death, mourns for him and Jonathan, and is made king over the southern region of Israel, called Judah.

DAY 104

2 SAMUEL 3–4

David rules from Hebron, fighting with Saul's son Ish-bosheth, king of the northern region, called Israel. In seven years, Ish-bosheth is murdered by two of his military captains.

DAY 105

2 SAMUEL 5–7

David becomes king over all Israel. He brings the ark of the covenant to Jerusalem and hopes to build a temple. God says no but promises an everlasting kingdom for David.

DAY 106

2 SAMUEL 8–10

David defeats many of Israel's enemies in battle. And he generously welcomes Saul's disabled grandson, Mephibosheth, to live in his palace.

DAY 107

2 SAMUEL 11–12

David takes his neighbor's beautiful wife, then has the man killed. David repents, but God says "the sword shall never depart" from his home. Solomon is later born to the woman, now married to David.

DAY 108

2 SAMUEL 13–14

David's sins lead to family problems. One son assaults a half sister, only to be killed by the girl's full brother, David's handsome and ambitious son Absalom.

DAY 109

2 SAMUEL 15–16

Absalom works to steal the kingship from his father, forcing David to run away from Jerusalem.

DAY 110

2 SAMUEL 17–18

Absalom is advised on how to fight his father, but his duplicitous counselor warns David of his son's plans. The two armies battle in the woods of Ephraim, where Absalom is killed. David mourns deeply for his lost child.

DAY 111

2 SAMUEL 19–20

David returns as king to Jerusalem, but the conflict with Absalom has created divisions in his kingdom.

DAY 112

2 SAMUEL 21–22

David must once again fight the Philistines, including descendants of the giant Goliath. He writes a psalm of praise to God for bringing him through safely.

DAY 113

2 SAMUEL 23–24

David counts his fighting men, apparently trusting his military strength over God's power. As punishment, he suffers the loss of seventy-thousand men.

KNOW YOUR BIBLE *MEN*

JOSEPH

DROP YOUR COAT AND RUN!

And she caught him by his garment, saying, "Lie with me."
And he left his garment in her hand and fled and got himself out.
GENESIS 39:12

†

Temptation isn't a sin. It is a liar. Temptation says, "Give in just this once. It's no big deal." But temptation changes people the way the ocean changes solid rock. It's never "just this once." Temptation wears you down, little by little, eroding your strength until, one day, you realize you're not who you used to be.

Joseph was smart, talented, and successful. Even though he was a foreign slave, he was so impressive that he ran his master's house. But do you know what was most impressive about Joseph? He knew how to get away from a bad situation. Look at how Joseph responded when Potiphar's wife tempted him. First, he recognized that giving in would be a sin (Genesis 39:9). Then, he dropped everything and ran (Genesis 39:12).

Memorizing Bible verses, asking God for help, and sharing your struggles with trusted Christian friends are all great ways to fight temptation. But sometimes, you just need to act like Joseph and run! Drop your phone. Shut your laptop. Leave the party. Do whatever you need to do to separate yourself from whatever tempts you. Use your legs to avoid giving in to sin. Flee and get yourself out!

Dear God, You know exactly what tempts me to sin. You know what my struggles are. Please help me to see how I can run from temptation. Thank You for always being with me.

1 KINGS

AUTHOR

Not stated and unknown; one early tradition claimed Jeremiah wrote 1 and 2 Kings.

DATE

Covering events from about 970 to 850 BC, 1 Kings was probably written sometime after the Babylonian destruction of Jerusalem in 586 BC.

IN TEN WORDS OR LESS

Israel divides into rival northern and southern nations.

DETAILS, PLEASE

King David, in declining health, names Solomon, his son with Bathsheba, successor. After David's death, God speaks to Solomon in a dream, offering him anything he'd like—and Solomon chooses wisdom. God gives Solomon great wisdom, along with much power and wealth. The new king soon builds God a permanent temple in Jerusalem, and the Lord visits Solomon again to promise blessings for obedience and trouble for disobedience. Sadly, Solomon's wisdom fails him, as he marries seven hundred women, many of them foreigners who turn his heart to idols. When Solomon dies, his son Rehoboam foolishly antagonizes the people of Israel, and ten northern tribes form their own nation under Jeroboam, a former official of Solomon's. Two southern tribes continue under Solomon's line in a nation called Judah. Jeroboam begins badly, initiating idol worship in the north; many wicked rulers follow. Judah will also have many poor leaders, though occasional kings, such as Asa and Jehoshaphat, follow the Lord. 1 Kings introduces the prophet Elijah, who confronts the evil King Ahab and Queen Jezebel of Israel regarding their worship of the false god Baal. In God's power, Elijah defeats 450 false prophets in a dramatic contest on Mount Carmel.

QUOTABLE

- The days of David drew near that he should die, and he charged his son Solomon, saying, "I am going the way of all the earth. Therefore be strong, and show yourself a man." (2:1–2)
- "Therefore give Your servant an understanding heart to judge Your people, that I may discern between good and bad. For who is able to judge this great people of Yours?" (3:9)
- "Hear me, O LORD, hear me, that this people may know that You are the LORD God and that You have turned their hearts back again." (18:37)

UNIQUE AND UNUSUAL

Scholars say 1 and 2 Kings were originally a single volume and were split in half to allow for copying onto normal-sized scrolls.

SO WHAT?

Solomon's example provides a strong warning: Even the most blessed person can drift from God and make big mistakes.

DAY 114

1 KINGS 1–2

David, now old and dying, announces that Solomon will follow him as king. When David dies, Solomon protects himself by killing several of his enemies.

DAY 115

1 KINGS 3–4

God offers Solomon anything he wants, and the new king requests wisdom. Pleased with this response, God also promises Solomon wealth and fame.

DAY 116

1 KINGS 5–7

Solomon builds the temple for God that his father, David, had hoped to build. The construction takes seven years; Solomon spends thirteen years building his own palace.

DAY 117

1 KINGS 8–9

Solomon brings the ark of the covenant to its permanent home in the Jerusalem temple. God warns that idolatry in Israel will lead to the beloved temple's ruin.

DAY 118

1 KINGS 10–11

Solomon becomes famous for his wisdom and wealth. But then he marries seven hundred women, who turn his heart toward idols. God raises up a rival, one of Solomon's officials named Jeroboam.

DAY 119

1 KINGS 12–13

After Solomon dies, his son Rehoboam becomes king. Rehoboam foolishly treats the people badly. Ten northern tribes break away and make Jeroboam their king.

DAY 120

1 KINGS 14–15

Israel, the northern kingdom, suffers under a series of evil kings. In Judah, the southern kingdom, Rehoboam and his son Abijah are wicked, but Abijah's son Asa follows God.

DAY 121

1 KINGS 16–17

Israel's poor leadership continues under several kings, the worst of all named Ahab. The prophet Elijah predicts a drought and raises a widow's son from the dead.

DAY 122

1 KINGS 18–19

Elijah confronts Ahab and his queen, Jezebel, for their Baal worship. Elijah defeats hundreds of false prophets on Mount Carmel. Then he calls Elisha to be prophet after him.

DAY 123

1 KINGS 20–21

King Ahab wants his neighbor's vineyard, so Queen Jezebel arranges to have the man killed. The prophet Elijah announces doom for the king and queen.

DAY 124

1 KINGS 22

King Ahab of Israel dies in battle and is replaced by his evil son Ahaziah; in Judah, Asa's son Jehoshaphat begins a good twenty-five-year reign.

2 KINGS

AUTHOR

Not stated and unknown; one early tradition claimed Jeremiah wrote 1 and 2 Kings.

DATE

Covering about three hundred years from the 800s BC on, 2 Kings was probably written sometime after the Babylonian destruction of Jerusalem in 586 BC.

IN TEN WORDS OR LESS

Both Jewish nations are destroyed for their disobedience to God.

DETAILS, PLEASE

The story of 1 Kings continues, with more bad rulers, a handful of good ones, some familiar prophets, and the ultimate loss of the two Jewish nations. Early in 2 Kings, Elijah becomes the second man (after Enoch in Genesis 5:24) to go straight to heaven without dying. His successor, Elisha, performs many miracles and shares God's word with the "average people" of Israel. The northern kingdom's rulers are entirely wicked, and Israel, under its last king, Hoshea, is "carried. . .away into Assyria" (17:6) in 722 BC. Judah, with occasional good kings such as Hezekiah and Josiah, lasts a few years longer—but in 586 BC the southern kingdom's capital of Jerusalem "was broken up" (25:4) by Babylonian armies under King Nebuchadnezzar. Besides taking everything valuable from the temple and the Jewish king's palace, the Babylonians also "carried away all Jerusalem and all the princes and all the mighty men of valor, even ten thousand captives, and all the craftsmen and metalworkers" (24:14). Ending on a slight up note, 2 Kings describes a new king of Babylon, Evil-merodach, showing kindness to Jehoiachin, the last real king of Judah, by giving him a place of honor in the Babylonian court.

QUOTABLE

- Behold, a chariot of fire and horses of fire appeared and parted them both apart, and Elijah went up by a whirlwind into heaven. (2:11)
- The LORD rejected all the descendants of Israel and afflicted them and delivered them into the hand of plunderers, until He had cast them out of His sight. (17:20)
- So Judah was carried away out of their land. (25:21)

UNIQUE AND UNUSUAL

Isaiah, who wrote a long prophecy that appears later in the Old Testament, is prominent in 2 Kings 19. One of Judah's best kings, Josiah, was only eight years old when he took the throne (22:1).

SO WHAT?

Both Israel and Judah found that there were terrible consequences to sin. Even bad examples can be helpful if we decide not to do the things that bring us trouble.

DAY 125

2 KINGS 1-3

The prophet Elijah is taken directly to heaven in a chariot of fire. His helper Elisha becomes the main prophet in Israel.

DAY 126

2 KINGS 4-5

Elisha performs many miracles: increasing a widow's oil supply, raising another woman's son from the dead, and curing a Syrian commander's leprosy.

DAY 127

2 KINGS 6-8

Elisha predicts the end of a Syrian siege of Israel and a seven-year famine. Meanwhile, Judah's kings, Jehoram and Ahaziah, act wickedly.

DAY 128

2 KINGS 9-10

Elisha anoints Jehu king of Israel. Jehu fulfills a prophecy of God by killing Ahab's wife, Jezebel, and their son, King Joram. Jehu then destroys Baal worship in Israel.

DAY 129

2 KINGS 11-13

A young royal in Judah, Joash (or Jehoash), becomes king. Early in his reign, he oversees revival and the repair of God's temple in Jerusalem.

DAY 130

2 KINGS 14-15

Many kings, all of them bad, rule over Israel. Some of Judah's kings are better, with Azariah (also known as Uzziah) and his son Jotham being generally good.

DAY 131

2 KINGS 16–17

Israel's many sins finally lead to the nation's punishment: an Assyrian invasion. The people of Israel are forced to leave their country, while outsiders replace them.

DAY 132

2 KINGS 18–19

Judah's godly King Hezekiah faces an invasion by a huge Assyrian army. The king's humble prayer leads God to destroy 185,000 enemy soldiers.

DAY 133

2 KINGS 20–21

Hezekiah gets a deadly disease and prays. The prophet Isaiah says God will give him fifteen more years to live. When Hezekiah dies, his son Manasseh is an evil king.

DAY 134

2 KINGS 22:1–23:30

Another young king, eight-year-old Josiah, leads Judah into respect for God and His laws. After a thirty-one-year reign, he dies in battle against Egypt.

DAY 135

2 KINGS 23:31–25:30

Judah's final four kings are wicked. God sends the Babylonians under King Nebuchadnezzar to invade the nation. Jerusalem is destroyed and many people carried away.

KNOW YOUR BIBLE *MEN*

MOSES

FAITH IN GOD'S PLANS

"So now, go. I am sending you to Pharaoh to bring
my people the Israelites out of Egypt."
Exodus 3:10 NIV

†

It was unlikely that Moses was going to amount to much. Though God had miraculously spared his life at birth and placed him in Pharaoh's family (Exodus 2:1–10), Moses squandered God's blessings. In a rage, he murdered an Egyptian slave master, then fled to the countryside to escape the punishment of Pharaoh, his own grandfather (Exodus 2:11–15). However, God miraculously spoke to Moses from a burning bush, calling him to be the leader of Israel. Despite Moses' flaws and sins, God chose this man to lead His people out of their slavery (Exodus 3:1–22).

Moses' story reveals that God uses sinful, imperfect people to do His work. While he was reluctant at first, Moses did have faith in God's plans (Hebrews 11:24–28). God is simply looking for a faithful, willing man who will follow His lead. Flawless men aren't expected—because they don't actually exist.

God already knows you're not perfect. He knows about your weaknesses and sin. He's called every one of us to love Him and our neighbors (Matthew 22:34–40). And sometimes God even asks us to do specific tasks, as he did with Moses. The question is this: Will you put your faith in Him, despite your flaws? Will you have a willing heart?

Dear God, thank You for using sinful, imperfect people like me. I will put my faith in Your plans for my life. Please help me to follow Your lead. Please use the blessings You've given me to help others.

1 CHRONICLES

AUTHOR

Not stated but traditionally attributed to Ezra the priest.

DATE

Covers the history of Israel from about 1010 BC (the death of King Saul) to about 970 BC (the death of King David).

IN TEN WORDS OR LESS KING

David's reign is detailed and analyzed.

DETAILS, PLEASE

1 Chronicles provides a history of Israel, going as far back as Adam. By the eleventh chapter, the story turns to Israel's greatest king, David, with special emphasis on his leadership of national worship. Another important focus is on God's promise that David would have an eternal kingly line through his descendant Jesus Christ.

QUOTABLE

- "I will settle him in My house and in My kingdom forever. And his throne shall be established forevermore." (17:14)

UNIQUE AND UNUSUAL

1 Chronicles covers much of the same information as 2 Samuel, but without some of the seedier aspects of David's life—such as his adultery with Bathsheba and the engineered killing of her husband, Uriah.

SO WHAT?

The positive spin of 1 Chronicles was designed to remind the Jews that despite their punishment for sin, they were still God's special people. When God makes a promise, He keeps it.

DAY 136

1 CHRONICLES 1–4

1 Chronicles covers many of the events of the books of Samuel and Kings. But it focuses on the nation of Judah, beginning with a history of Jacob's son Judah through King David.

DAY 137

1 CHRONICLES 5–7

Quick histories of the other sons of Jacob are provided, with an emphasis on the line of Levi, which produced Israel's priests.

DAY 138

1 CHRONICLES 8–10

The tribe of Benjamin, family line of Israel's first king (Saul), is highlighted. Saul's death in a battle against the Philistines is described.

DAY 139

1 CHRONICLES 11–14

David becomes king and makes Jerusalem his capital. He brings the ark of the covenant to the city with great joy—but a man named Uzza dies for touching the ark.

DAY 140

1 CHRONICLES 15–17

David moves the ark of the covenant into his capital of Jerusalem, with great celebration and sacrifice. God promises David a "kingdom forever."

DAY 141

1 CHRONICLES 18–21

David makes his kingdom strong with military victories. But he sins when he decides to count his fighting men. God punishes Israel with a three-day plague.

DAY 142

1 CHRONICLES 22–24

David prepares material for God's temple, which his son Solomon will build. David names Solomon his successor as king.

DAY 143

1 CHRONICLES 25–27

David organizes worship leaders, temple workers, and other officers for the nation of Israel.

DAY 144

1 CHRONICLES 28–29

David tells Israel that Solomon will be the next king. He urges the people to support Solomon in building God's temple. Then David dies after a forty-year reign and Solomon takes the throne.

2 CHRONICLES

AUTHOR

Not stated but traditionally attributed to Ezra the priest.

DATE

Covers Israelite history from about 970 BC (the accession of King Solomon) to the 500s BC (when exiled Jews returned to Jerusalem).

IN TEN WORDS OR LESS

The history of Israel from Solomon to division to destruction.

DETAILS, PLEASE

David's son Solomon is made king, builds the temple, and becomes one of the most prominent rulers ever. But when he dies, the Jewish nation divides. In the remainder of 2 Chronicles, the various kings of the relatively godlier southern nation of Judah are profiled right down to the destruction of Jerusalem by the Babylonians. The book ends with the Persian king Cyrus allowing Jews to rebuild the devastated temple.

QUOTABLE

- "O Lord God of Israel, there is no God like You in heaven or on earth, who keeps Your covenant and shows mercy to Your servants who walk before You with all their hearts." (6:14)

UNIQUE AND UNUSUAL

Continuing the positive spin of 1 Chronicles (the two books were originally one), 2 Chronicles ends with two verses that exactly repeat the first three verses of Ezra.

SO WHAT?

God's punishment isn't intended to hurt people but to bring them back to Him.

DAY 145

2 CHRONICLES 1–4

In a vision, God offers Solomon anything he wishes; the new king chooses wisdom. In the fourth year of his reign, Solomon begins building God's temple.

DAY 146

2 CHRONICLES 5–7

Solomon finishes God's temple. He brings in the ark of the covenant, then preaches and prays. God promises blessing for obedience and warns of punishment for disobedience.

DAY 147

2 CHRONICLES 8–9

As God had promised, Solomon is a wise, famous, and wealthy king. The visiting queen of Sheba is amazed at Solomon. After reigning for forty years, he dies.

DAY 148

2 CHRONICLES 10–13

Solomon's son Rehoboam becomes king and foolishly angers the Israelites. Ten northern tribes break away and name their own king, Jeroboam.

DAY 149

2 CHRONICLES 14–18

Separate Jewish kingdoms, Israel and Judah, go through years of conflict under a series of often bad kings.

DAY 150

2 CHRONICLES 19–21

Judah's King Jehoshaphat rules well, restoring good worship and fighting off an invasion. But he is followed by a wicked son, Jehoram.

DAY 151

2 CHRONICLES 22–24

Jehoram's son Ahaziah rules wickedly and dies in battle. A seven-year-old son, Joash, is made king. His forty-year reign starts well, but he becomes sinful and is murdered.

DAY 152

2 CHRONICLES 25–28

Judah faces many battles, even with the northern kingdom of Israel. Uzziah (also called Azariah) rules well but gets leprosy after pridefully entering the temple.

DAY 153

2 CHRONICLES 29–30

A very good king, Hezekiah, rules Judah, overseeing a spiritual revival, the return of worship in the temple, and the keeping of the Passover.

DAY 154

2 CHRONICLES 31–33

Hezekiah destroys idols in Judah, then prays for help to resist an Assyrian invasion. His son Manasseh follows him as king, but he does "evil in the sight of the LORD."

DAY 155

2 CHRONICLES 34–36

Judah's history winds down with one good king (Josiah) and several wicked ones, before the nation is invaded and its people carried away by the Babylonians.

EZRA

AUTHOR

Not stated but traditionally attributed to Ezra the priest (7:11).

DATE

Approximately 530 BC to the mid-400s BC.

IN TEN WORDS OR LESS

Spiritual renewal begins after the Jews return from exile.

DETAILS, PLEASE

About a half century after Babylonians sacked Jerusalem and carried Jews into captivity, Persia is the new world power. King Cyrus allows a group of exiles to return to Judah to rebuild the temple. Some 42,000 people return and resettle the land. About seventy years later, Ezra is part of a smaller group that also returns. He teaches the law to the people, who have fallen away from God to the point of intermarrying with nearby pagan nations, something that was strictly forbidden by Moses (Deuteronomy 7:1–3).

QUOTABLE

- Ezra had prepared his heart to seek the law of the Lord and to do it and to teach statutes and judgments in Israel. (7:10)

UNIQUE AND UNUSUAL

Though the Bible reports that "the Lord, the God of Israel, says that He hates divorce" (Malachi 2:16), Ezra urged Jewish men to separate from their foreign wives.

SO WHAT?

In Ezra, God shows His willingness to offer a second chance—allowing a nation that had been punished for disobedience to have a fresh start. Guess what? He's still in the second-chance business.

DAY 156

EZRA 1–3

Cyrus, the king of Persia who conquered Babylon,
allows many Jews to return to Judah. More than forty thousand
go and begin laying a foundation for the ruined temple.

DAY 157

EZRA 4–6

Enemies try to stop the Jews' rebuilding of the temple.
But a new king of Persia, Darius, allows them to continue.
The work is finished seventy years after the Babylonian destruction.

DAY 158

EZRA 7–8

Ezra, an exiled priest, travels to Jerusalem
"to teach statutes and judgments in Israel."

DAY 159

EZRA 9–10

Ezra is upset to learn that many Jews have
broken God's law by marrying foreign women.
He urges them to leave their wives, and many do.

NEHEMIAH

AUTHOR

"The words of Nehemiah" (1:1), though Jewish tradition says those words were put on paper by Ezra.

DATE

Approximately 445 BC.

IN TEN WORDS OR LESS

Returning Jewish exiles rebuild the broken walls of Jerusalem.

DETAILS, PLEASE

Nehemiah serves as "the king's cupbearer" (1:11) in Shushan, Persia. As a Jew, he's disturbed to learn that even though exiles have been back in Judah for nearly a hundred years, they have not rebuilt the city's walls, devastated by the Babylonians in 586 BC. Nehemiah asks and receives the king's permission to return to Jerusalem, where he leads a team of builders—against much pagan opposition—in reconstructing the walls in only fifty-two days. The quick work on the project shocks the Jews' enemies, who "perceived that this work was done by our God" (6:16).

QUOTABLE

- Remember me, my God, for good, according to all that I have done for this people. (5:19)

UNIQUE AND UNUSUAL

Indignant over some fellow Jews' intermarriage with pagans, Nehemiah "cursed them, and struck some of them, and plucked out their hair" (13:25).

SO WHAT?

Nehemiah's success in rebuilding Jerusalem's walls provides many leadership principles for today—especially his consistent focus on prayer.

DAY 160

NEHEMIAH 1–3

Nehemiah, an exiled Jew, works for the Persian king Artaxerxes. Nehemiah asks and receives the king's approval to go to Jerusalem to rebuild its broken walls.

DAY 161

NEHEMIAH 4–6

Enemies of the Jews try to stop the rebuilding work, but the walls are done in fifty-two days. Nehemiah says "this work was done by our God."

DAY 162

NEHEMIAH 7–9

The priest Ezra appears again, reading and explaining God's law to the people. The Jews fast and repent of their sins.

DAY 163

NEHEMIAH 10–11

The people promise to live up to their covenant with God. They call a curse on themselves if they fail.

DAY 164

NEHEMIAH 12–13

The Jews celebrate the new walls of Jerusalem. But Nehemiah points out things they've done wrong—like allowing foreigners in the temple and working on the Sabbath. He prays, "Remember me, O my God, for good!"

ESTHER

AUTHOR

Not stated but perhaps Ezra or Nehemiah.

DATE

Approximately 486–465 BC, during the reign of King Ahasuerus of Persia. Esther became queen around 479 BC.

IN TEN WORDS OR LESS

Beautiful Jewish girl becomes queen, saves fellow Jews from slaughter.

DETAILS, PLEASE

In a nationwide beauty contest, young Esther becomes queen of Persia without revealing her Jewish heritage. When a royal official plots to kill every Jew in the country, Esther risks her own life to request the king's protection. The king, pleased with Esther, is shocked by his official's plan and has the man hanged—while decreeing that the Jews should defend themselves against the planned slaughter. Esther's people prevail and commemorate the event with a holiday called Purim.

QUOTABLE

- Esther obtained favor in the sight of all those who saw her. (2:15)
- "Who knows whether you have come to the kingdom for such a time as this?" (4:14)

UNIQUE AND UNUSUAL

God's name is never mentioned in the book of Esther. Neither is prayer, though Esther asks her fellow Jews to fast for her before she approaches the king (4:16).

SO WHAT?

When we find ourselves in bad situations, it may be for the same reason Esther did—to accomplish something good.

DAY 165

ESTHER 1–3

In Persia, the king makes a beautiful Jewish exile named Esther his queen. A royal advisor, Haman, plots against the Jews.

DAY 166

ESTHER 4–6

Approaching the Persian king without an invitation can be punished by death. But Esther bravely enters his presence to plead for her people.

DAY 167

ESTHER 7–10

Haman is executed, and the Jews are allowed to defend themselves against his murderous plot. A holiday called Purim reminds Jews of Esther's bravery.

KNOW YOUR BIBLE MEN

AARON

LEAD OR CAVE?

He took what they handed him and made it into an idol cast in the shape of a calf, fashioning it with a tool. Then they said, "These are your gods, Israel, who brought you up out of Egypt."
EXODUS 32:4 NIV

†

Insecurity. Peer pressure. Caving in. Aaron was supposed to be a leader, yet this is his legacy.

Aaron was Moses' older brother and the first high priest for Israel (Exodus 28:1). He was never the top dog, but the one time he was left in charge, Aaron created an idol, led a sinful revelry, and blamed the Israelites for his own poor choices (Exodus 32:1–24). Given the chance to lead, Aaron caved and played the victim.

You will have opportunities to lead too. You may be asked to head up a group at school or church. You may be asked to lead your team through a practice or your band through a rehearsal. Or you might simply be asked to watch over a younger kid for a while. What will you do when you're in charge? Will you do the right thing? Or, like Aaron, will you cave in to foolish pressures?

God is loving and merciful even when we cave. Israel's unfaithfulness under Aaron made Him angry enough to destroy them—but God chose to hold back His harshest punishment (Exodus 32:9–14). He does the same for all who believe in Jesus (Romans 6:23). Still, isn't it obvious that it's better not to cave in?

If you've placed your faith in Jesus, God may ask you to be a leader someday. What will you do when it's your turn?

Dear God, please help me to rely on Your strength when I feel insecure or pressured to sin. Help me to be a leader who always reflects Your goodness.

JOB

AUTHOR

Not stated.

DATE

Unclear, but many believe Job is one of the oldest stories in the Bible, perhaps from approximately 2000 BC.

IN TEN WORDS OR LESS

God allows human suffering for His own purposes.

DETAILS, PLEASE

Head of a large family, Job is a wealthy farmer from a place called Uz. He's "perfect and upright" (1:1)—so much so, that God calls Satan's attention to him. The devil, unimpressed, asks and receives God's permission to attack Job's possessions—and wipes out thousands of sheep, camels, oxen, donkeys, and worst of all, Job's ten children. Despite Satan's attack, Job keeps his faith. Satan then receives God's permission to attack Job's health—but in spite of terrible physical suffering, Job refuses to "curse God and die" as his wife suggests (2:9). Before long, though, Job begins to question why God would allow him—a good man—to suffer so severely. Job's suffering is worsened by the arrival of four "friends" who begin to accuse him of causing his own trouble by secret sin. "Is not your wickedness great?" asks Eliphaz the Temanite (22:5). In the end, God Himself speaks, vindicating Job before his friends and also addressing the overarching issue of human suffering. God doesn't explain Job's suffering but asks a series of questions that shows His vast knowledge—implying that Job should simply trust God's way. And Job does, telling God, "I know that You can do everything" (42:2). By story's end, God has restored Job's health, possessions, and family, giving him ten more children.

QUOTABLE

- "Naked I came out of my mother's womb and naked I shall return there. The LORD gave and the LORD has taken away. Blessed be the name of the LORD." (1:21)
- "Man who is born of a woman is of few days and full of trouble." (14:1)
- "You are all miserable comforters." (16:2)
- "I hate myself and repent in dust and ashes." (42:6)

UNIQUE AND UNUSUAL

The book of Job pictures Satan coming into God's presence (1:6). It also gives a clear Old Testament hint of Jesus' work when Job says, "I know that my Redeemer lives and that He shall stand at the latter day on the earth" (19:25).

SO WHAT?

Trouble isn't necessarily a sign of sin in a person's life. It may be something God allows to draw us closer to Him.

DAY 168

JOB 1–5

A good man named Job loses his children, his wealth, and his health in a short time. He doesn't realize that God has allowed Satan's attacks to prove Job's goodness. Three friends arrive to comfort him. Soon, though, Eliphaz accuses the righteous Job of needing correction for sin.

DAY 169

JOB 6–10

Job mourns his losses and seeks pity from God and his friends. Bildad, instead of offering pity, accuses him of hypocrisy. Job responds with faith and grief.

DAY 170

JOB 11–14

Job's friend Zophar accuses Job of lying. Job defends himself but seems to be losing hope. He pleads with his friends to be silent and not "contend for God."

DAY 171

JOB 15–19

Eliphaz accuses Job of hidden sins. Job cries, "You are all miserable comforters." Though he feels like God is attacking him, Job says, "I know that my Redeemer lives."

DAY 172

JOB 20–24

Job longs to talk with God, to have an opportunity to present his case before the Lord.

DAY 173

JOB 25–31

Job still defends himself, saying he had even made a promise with his eyes not to look at young women. He knows that God can see his innocence.

DAY 174

JOB 32–37

Another man arrives to criticize everyone. Elihu complains that Job "justified himself rather than God" and the three friends, "because they had found no answer and yet had condemned Job."

DAY 175

JOB 38–42

Job finally hears from God, who asks questions that Job can't answer. Job admits God can do as He pleases. When Job repents and prays for his friends, God restores Job's wealth and family.

PSALMS

AUTHORS

Various, with nearly half attributed to King David. Other names noted include Solomon, Moses, Asaph, Ethan, and the sons of Korah. Many psalms don't mention an author.

DATE

Approximately the 1400s BC (Moses' time) through the 500s BC (the time of the Jews' Babylonian exile).

IN TEN WORDS OR LESS

Ancient Jewish songbook showcases prayers, praise—and complaints—to God.

DETAILS, PLEASE

Over several centuries, God led various individuals to compose emotionally charged poems—of which 150 were later compiled into the book we know as Psalms. Many of the psalms are described as "of David," meaning they could be by, for, or about Israel's great king. Highlights of the book include the "shepherd psalm" (23), which describes God as protector and provider; David's cry for forgiveness after his sin with Bathsheba (51); psalms of praise (100 is a powerful example); and the celebration of scripture found in Psalm 119, with almost all of the 176 verses making some reference to God's laws, statutes, commandments, precepts, word, and the like. Some psalms, called "imprecatory," call for God's judgment on enemies (see Psalms 69 and 109, for example). Many psalms express agony of spirit on the writer's part—but nearly every psalm returns to the theme of praise to God. That's the way the book of Psalms ends: "Let everything that has breath praise the Lord. Praise the Lord" (150:6).

QUOTABLE

- LORD, our Lord, how excellent is Your name in all the earth. (8:1)

- The Lord is my shepherd. I shall not want. (23:1)
- Create in me a clean heart, O God, and renew a right spirit within me. (51:10)
- Your word have I hidden in my heart, that I might not sin against You. (119:11)
- I will lift up my eyes to the hills. Where does my help come from? My help comes from the Lord, who made heaven and earth. (121:1–2)
- Behold, how good and how pleasant it is for brothers to dwell together in unity! (133:1)

UNIQUE AND UNUSUAL

The book of Psalms is the Bible's longest, in terms of both number of chapters (150) and total word count. It contains the longest chapter in the Bible (Psalm 119, with 176 verses) and the shortest (Psalm 117, with 2 verses). Psalm 118 is also the midpoint of the Protestant Bible, with 594 chapters before it and 594 after.

SO WHAT?

The psalms run the gamut of human emotion—which is why so many people turn to them in times of both joy and sadness.

DAY 176

PSALMS 1–10

God "knows the way of the righteous," is a shield to the persecuted, and a refuge in times of trouble. Though He created the stars, He thinks much of people.

DAY 177

PSALMS 11–18

Fools believe there is no God; evil talkers are kept out of His presence. The psalm writer praises the Lord's faithfulness to His promises to David and his family.

DAY 178

PSALMS 19–27

All creation shows God's glory. The Lord is a shepherd to His people. With God as "my light and my salvation," there is no need to fear.

DAY 179

PSALMS 28–34

God's anger is brief, but "joy comes in the morning." Confession of sin brings forgiveness and happiness. God is near to the brokenhearted and humble.

DAY 180

PSALMS 35–39

We should not envy evildoers, who will soon fall. Meek people will inherit the earth. God does not leave His children on their own.

DAY 181

PSALMS 40–47

Wait patiently for God, and He will listen. The Lord honors those who help the poor. He is His people's refuge and strength, "a very present help in trouble."

DAY 182

PSALMS 48–55

Call on God in the day of trouble, and He will deliver you. Humble, personal admission of sin—as of David's with Bathsheba—God "will not despise."

DAY 183

PSALMS 56–65

Look to God for help in trouble, "for useless is the help of man." Power belongs to God.

DAY 184

PSALMS 66–71

Praise God in song for His powerful works. Don't treasure sin in your heart, or else "the Lord will not hear." God is our hope; we go on in His strength.

DAY 185

PSALMS 72–77

The wicked may seem to succeed, but they face a terrible end. The Lord should be feared: "Who is so great a God as our God?"

DAY 186

PSALMS 78–82

God blessed and performed miracles for the ancient Israelites, then had to discipline them for sinning. He said sadly, "Oh that My people had listened to Me."

DAY 187

PSALMS 83–89

It is better to be a doorkeeper in God's temple than to live in "the tents of wickedness." The Lord loves Zion, Jerusalem, the "city of God."

DAY 188

PSALMS 90–99

The human lifespan is seventy or eighty years, so Moses asked God to "teach us to number our days." It is good to thank God and sing His praises.

DAY 189

PSALMS 100–105

God is good to forgive sins, heal diseases, and redeem our lives from destruction. It is good to remember "His marvelous works."

DAY 190

PSALMS 106–109

In spite of ancient Israel's many sinful failures, "many times [God] delivered them." His mercy "is great above the heavens."

DAY 191

PSALMS 110–118

God's people owe Him praise, thanks, and love: "Not to us, O Lord, not to us, but to Your name give glory, for Your mercy, and for Your truth's sake."

DAY 192

PSALM 119

The Bible's longest chapter (176 verses) praises God's Word, using names like "the law of the Lord," "testimonies," "precepts," "statutes," and "commandments."

DAY 193

PSALMS 120–134

These "songs of degrees" were sung by Israelites going up to Jerusalem. When God's people trust in Him, they are "as Mount Zion, which cannot be removed but abides forever."

DAY 194

PSALMS 135–142

God's mercy to His people lasts forever. So do His knowledge and thoughts of His people: "how great is the sum of them!"

DAY 195

PSALMS 143–150

People, angels, and all of creation are called to sing praise to God. "Let everything that has breath praise the Lord."

KNOW YOUR BIBLE *MEN*

GIDEON

TALKING WITH GOD

"If the LORD is with us, then why has all this happened to us? And where are all His miracles that our fathers told us of, saying, 'Did not the LORD bring us up from Egypt?'"
JUDGES 6:13

†

Have you ever wanted to ask God, "Why did this happen?" A young Israelite named Gideon did exactly that.

The book of Judges describes a long series of Israel's failures. They were stuck in a cycle of bad decisions and harsh consequences. During this dark time, Gideon became a leader in Israel. The neighboring nation of Midian had besieged God's people, destroyed their crops, and stole their cattle. Israel was starving. It couldn't have been easy for Gideon.

Wisely, he never stopped talking with God. Gideon even asked God the question that was on everyone's mind, "Why did this happen?" God responded by revealing an ingenious plan for Gideon to fool the Midianites. They drove thousands of enemy soldiers out of their land with only three hundred Israelite fighters (Judges 7).

What does Gideon's story tell us about God? For one thing, that we don't need to be afraid to ask Him hard questions. It's okay to tell God exactly how you feel, especially when you're facing overwhelming challenges. Gideon's story demonstrates that God cares about the suffering of His people—including you. You serve a very wise God. What will you ask Him?

Dear God, thank You for listening to my questions. Please explain to me why I'm struggling with my current problems—and help me to trust You to create ways around these things that overwhelm me. Please lead me into a new day like You did for Gideon and the Israelites.

PROVERBS

AUTHORS

Primarily Solomon (1:1), with sections attributed to "the wise" (22:17), Agur (30:1), and King Lemuel (31:1). Little is known of the latter two.

DATE

Solomon reigned approximately 970–930 BC. The staff of King Hezekiah, who lived about two hundred years later, "copied out" the latter chapters of the book we have today (25:1).

IN TEN WORDS OR LESS

Pithy, memorable sayings encourage people to pursue wisdom.

DETAILS, PLEASE

Proverbs doesn't have a story line—it's simply a collection of practical tips for living. Mainly from the pen of King Solomon, the wisest human being ever (in 1 Kings 3:12 God said, "I have given you a wise and understanding heart so that there has been none like you before you, nor shall any arise like you after you"), the proverbs speak to issues such as work, money, sex, temptation, drinking, laziness, discipline, and child rearing. Underlying each proverb is the truth that "the fear of the Lord is the beginning of knowledge" (1:7).

QUOTABLE

- Trust in the Lord with all your heart and do not lean on your own understanding. (3:5)
- Go to the ant, you sluggard! Consider her ways and be wise. (6:6)
- A wise son makes a glad father, but a foolish son is the heaviness of his mother. (10:1)
- As a jewel of gold in a swine's snout, so is a fair woman who is without discretion. (11:22)

- He who spares his rod hates his son, but he who loves him disciplines him promptly. (13:24)
- A soft answer turns away wrath, but harsh words stir up anger. (15:1)
- Commit your works to the Lord and your thoughts shall be established. (16:3)
- Even a fool, when he remains silent, is counted wise. (17:28)
- The name of the Lord is a strong tower. The righteous runs into it and is safe. (18:10)
- Wine is a mocker; strong drink is raging. (20:1)
- A good name is rather to be chosen than great riches. (22:1)
- Do not answer a fool according to his foolishness, lest you also be like him. (26:4)
- Faithful are the wounds of a friend. (27:6)

UNIQUE AND UNUSUAL

The final chapter of Proverbs includes a long poem in praise of wives, rather unusual for that time and culture.

SO WHAT?

Wisdom, as Proverbs 4:7 indicates, "is the principal thing. . .with all your getting, get understanding." If you need help with that, just ask God (James 1:5).

DAY 196

PROVERBS 1-5

Solomon urges his sons to search for wisdom "as for hidden treasures." The fear of the Lord is the "beginning of knowledge"; wise words "are life to those who find them."

DAY 197

PROVERBS 6-9

Laziness, pride, and dishonesty destroy people. Wisdom cries out, "whoever finds me finds life and shall obtain favor from the LORD."

DAY 198

PROVERBS 10-14

Righteousness and wickedness stand in contrast to each other: "Evil pursues sinners, but good shall be repaid to the righteous."

DAY 199

PROVERBS 15-19

People must choose between good and evil: "The LORD is far from the wicked, but He hears the prayer of the righteous."

DAY 200

PROVERBS 20–23

Wisdom offers warnings: "Wine is a mocker," "He who loves pleasure shall be a poor man," "The borrower is servant to the lender," "Make no friendship with an angry man."

DAY 201

PROVERBS 24–28

Wisdom provides instruction: "A man of knowledge increases strength," "If your enemy is hungry, give him bread to eat," "Where there is no talebearer, the strife ceases."

DAY 202

PROVERBS 29–31

A good woman sets an example for everyone: "She looks well to the ways of her household and does not eat the bread of idleness."

ECCLESIASTES

AUTHOR

Not stated but probably Solomon. The author is identified as "the son of David" (1:1) and "king in Jerusalem" (1:12) and says he had "more wisdom than all those who have been before me" (1:16).

DATE

900s BC.

IN TEN WORDS OR LESS

Apart from God, life is empty and unsatisfying.

DETAILS, PLEASE

A king pursues the things of this world, only to find them unfulfilling. Learning, pleasure, work, laughter—"all is vanity" (1:2). The king also laments the inequities of life: People live, work hard, and die, only to leave their belongings to someone else; the wicked prosper over the righteous; the poor are oppressed. Nevertheless, the king realizes "the conclusion of the whole matter: Fear God, and keep His commandments, for this is the whole duty of man" (12:13).

QUOTABLE

- All the rivers run into the sea, yet the sea is not full; to the place from where the rivers come, there they return again. (1:7)
- And whatever my eyes desired, I did not keep from them. I did not withhold my heart from any joy, for my heart rejoiced in all my labor. And this was my portion for all my labor. Then I looked at all the works that my hands had done, and on the labor that I had labored to do, and behold, all was vanity and vexation of spirit, and there was no profit under the sun. (2:10–11)

- There is a season for everything and a time for every purpose under heaven. (3:1)
- Remember now your Creator in the days of your youth. (12:1)

UNIQUE AND UNUSUAL

The book's generally negative tone makes some readers wonder if Solomon wrote it late in life, after his hundreds of wives led him to stray from God.

SO WHAT?

Life doesn't always make sense. . .but there's still a God who understands.

DAY 203

ECCLESIASTES 1–6

A "Preacher, the son of David, king in Jerusalem," seeks meaning in wealth and pleasure, but finds "vanity" and "vexation of spirit."

DAY 204

ECCLESIASTES 7–12

The Preacher realizes that on earth, "all is vanity," so humanity's duty is to "fear God and keep His commandments."

KNOW YOUR BIBLE *MEN*

SAMSON

WHAT COULD HAVE BEEN

And Samson called to the Lord and said, "O Lord God, remember me, I ask You. And strengthen me, I ask You, only this once, O God, that I may at once take vengeance on the Philistines for my two eyes."
Judges 16:28

†

Samson's life is a cautionary tale. Like a professional athlete who throws away his career with drugs and alcohol, Samson let his lust and temper destroy him. He'd been appointed to be a judge in Israel—a leader the people desperately needed during a lawless, evil time. His birth was heralded by an angel (Judges 13:2–5). God even gave Samson supernatural strength (Judges 14:19; 16:3). He was feared by Israel's enemies. Samson could have been one of Israel's most powerful and effective leaders.

Yet, "could've been" is how Samson is remembered. After being blinded and publicly humiliated, God allowed Samson to use his strength and temper one last time to take vengeance on the Philistines. It was a sad ending to a gifted life.

What are you doing with the gifts God has given you? What tempts you to sin? Are you on the path toward "could've been"? Allow Samson's story to work in you. In prayer, ask God to help you find the answers to these questions. Then, make whatever changes are necessary to follow God again. Because He is so good, God still used Samson in the end. But what could have been?

Heavenly Father, please work in my heart and mind. Help me to turn away from sin and use my life to honor You. May my life be marked by a persistent pursuit of You, not "what could've been."

SONG OF SOLOMON

AUTHOR

Solomon (1:1), though some wonder if the song "of Solomon" is like the psalms "of David"—which could mean they are by, for, or about him.

DATE

Solomon ruled around 970–930 BC.

IN TEN WORDS OR LESS

Married love is a beautiful thing worth celebrating.

DETAILS, PLEASE

A dark-skinned beauty is marrying the king, and both are thrilled. "Behold, you are beautiful, my love. Behold, you are beautiful. You have doves' eyes," he tells her (1:15). "Behold, you are beautiful, my beloved, yes, pleasant. Also our bed is green," she responds (1:16). Through eight chapters and 117 verses, the two lovers admire each other's physical beauty, expressing their love and devotion.

QUOTABLE

- Let him kiss me with the kisses of his mouth. For your love is better than wine. (1:2)
- I am the rose of Sharon and the lily of the valleys. (2:1)
- He brought me to the banqueting house, and his banner over me was love. (2:4)
- Behold, you are beautiful, my love. Behold, you are beautiful. You have doves' eyes within your hair. Your hair is like a flock of goats that appear from Mount Gilead. (4:1)
- Many waters cannot quench love, nor can the floods drown it. (8:7)

UNIQUE AND UNUSUAL

Like the book of Esther, Song of Solomon never mentions the name of God.

SO WHAT?

God made marriage for the husband and wife's enjoyment—and that marital love can be a picture of God's joy in His people.

DAY 205

SONG OF SOLOMON 1–8

A handsome young king and his beautiful, dark-skinned bride celebrate their love for each other.

ISAIAH

AUTHOR

Isaiah, son of Amoz (1:1).

DATE

Around 740–700 BC, starting "in the year that king Uzziah died" (6:1).

IN TEN WORDS OR LESS

A coming Messiah will save people from their sins.

DETAILS, PLEASE

Like most prophets, Isaiah announced the bad news of punishment for sin. But he also described a coming Messiah who would be "wounded for our transgressions. . .bruised for our iniquities. . .and with His lashes we are healed" (53:5). Called to the ministry through a stunning vision of God in heaven (chapter 6), Isaiah wrote a book that some call "the fifth Gospel" for its predictions of the birth, life, and death of Jesus Christ some seven hundred years later. These prophecies of redemption balance the depressing promises of God's discipline against Judah and Jerusalem, which were overrun by Babylonian armies about a century later. Isaiah's prophecy ends with a long section (chapters 40–66) describing God's restoration of Israel, His promised salvation, and His eternal kingdom.

QUOTABLE

- "Holy, holy, holy, is the LORD of hosts. The whole earth is full of His glory." (6:3)
- "Behold, a virgin shall conceive and bear a son, and shall call His name Immanuel." (7:14)
- For a Child is born to us, a Son is given to us, and the government shall be on His shoulder. And His name shall be called Wonderful, Counselor, the Mighty God, the Everlasting Father, the Prince of Peace. (9:6)

- We all like sheep have gone astray. We have turned, each one, to his own way, and the LORD has laid on Him the iniquity of us all. (53:6)

UNIQUE AND UNUSUAL

Isaiah had two children with strange, prophetic names. Shear-jashub (7:3) means "a remnant shall return," and Maher-shalal-hash-baz (8:3) means "haste to the spoil." Shear-jashub's name carried God's promise that exiled Jews would one day return home. Maher-shalal-hash-baz's name assured the king of Judah that his country's enemies would be handled by Assyrian armies.

SO WHAT?

Early in His ministry, Jesus said He fulfilled the prophecies of Isaiah: "The Lord has anointed Me to preach good news to the meek. He has sent Me to bind up the brokenhearted, to proclaim liberty to the captives, and the opening of the prison to those who are bound, to proclaim the acceptable year of the Lord" (61:1–2). It's amazing how much God cares about us!

DAY 206

ISAIAH 1–4

Isaiah, a prophet to Judah during the reigns of several kings, learns both of God's coming judgment and His blessing for the "last days."

DAY 207

ISAIAH 5–7

Isaiah sees an incredible vision of God on His throne. The prophet shares the message of a virgin-born baby to be called Immanuel, or "God with us."

DAY 208

ISAIAH 8–10

Isaiah's prediction of an Assyrian invasion is offset by the prophecy of the birth of a child called "Wonderful, Counselor, the Mighty God, the Everlasting Father, the Prince of Peace."

DAY 209

ISAIAH 11–14

A future kingdom, built on God's promise to David, will see "the cow and the bear" eating peacefully together. Before then, God will destroy powerful Babylon.

DAY 210

ISAIAH 15–19

God will judge and punish Moab, Damascus, and Egypt. But someday He will heal and draw many of these people to Himself.

DAY 211

ISAIAH 20–23

Warnings to godless nations are joined by a prophecy of doom toward Jerusalem: "a day of trouble and of trampling and of perplexity by the Lord GOD."

DAY 212

ISAIAH 24–27

A coming judgment on the whole earth will be followed by a day when God "will swallow up death in victory" and "wipe away tears from all faces."

DAY 213

ISAIAH 28–31

Isaiah says an Assyrian invasion of the northern kingdom of Israel is coming. He warns Judah against asking Egypt for military help.

DAY 214

ISAIAH 32–35

Isaiah looks ahead to the far future, when "a king shall reign in righteousness," when God destroys all His enemies, and when "the ransomed of the LORD" return to Jerusalem.

DAY 215

ISAIAH 36–39

Assyrians invade Judah. King Hezekiah prays, Isaiah carries God's message of protection, and the angel of the Lord destroys 185,000 enemy soldiers.

DAY 216

ISAIAH 40–42

Isaiah prophesies of John the Baptist ("him who cries in the wilderness") and Jesus ("to open the blind eyes, to bring out the prisoners from the prison").

DAY 217

ISAIAH 43–45

Judah faces captivity in Babylon, but Isaiah prophesies help from the Persian king Cyrus. It is only in the Lord, however, that "all the descendants of Israel" will be made right.

DAY 218

ISAIAH 46–48

God will judge Babylon for its pride. But the prideful Israelites will also face His punishment before being restored to their land.

DAY 219

ISAIAH 49–51

A coming Holy One, who will give His "back to those who strike," will buy back God's people from sin. One day, they will "come to Zion with singing."

DAY 220

ISAIAH 52–56

The Holy One will be "wounded for our transgressions" and "bruised for our iniquities." He will carry the sins of many and provide an everlasting salvation.

DAY 221

ISAIAH 57–59

God's people are warned against idolatry, pride, fake worship, and allowing or pursuing injustice against others. A deliverer is promised.

DAY 222

ISAIAH 60–63

A coming Deliverer will bring Jews and Gentiles together. God will restore the destroyed Jerusalem as "a crown of glory."

DAY 223

ISAIAH 64–66

God is planning "new heavens and a new earth" where evil people will be no more. It will be a place of peace, comfort, and goodness.

JEREMIAH

AUTHOR

Jeremiah (1:1), with the assistance of Baruch, a scribe (36:4).

DATE

Approximately 585 BC.

IN TEN WORDS OR LESS

After years of sinful behavior, Judah will be punished.

DETAILS, PLEASE

Called to the ministry as a boy (1:6), Jeremiah prophesies bad news to Judah: "'Behold, I will bring a nation upon you from afar, O house of Israel,' says the LORD" (5:15). Jeremiah is mocked for his prophecies, occasionally beaten, and imprisoned in a muddy well (chapter 38). But his words come true with the Babylonian invasion of chapter 52.

QUOTABLE

- "Behold, as the clay is in the potter's hand, so are you in My hand, O house of Israel." (18:6)

UNIQUE AND UNUSUAL

The book of Jeremiah that we read is apparently an expanded, second version of a destroyed first draft. King Jehoiakim, angry with Jeremiah for his dire prophecies, cut the scroll with a penknife and "cast it into the fire that was on the hearth" (36:23). At God's command, Jeremiah produced a second scroll with additional material (36:32).

SO WHAT?

Through Jeremiah, God gave Judah some forty years to repent. God "is long-suffering toward us, not willing that any should perish but that all should come to repentance" (2 Peter 3:9).

DAY 224

JEREMIAH 1–3

God calls young Jeremiah to warn Judah of its sin. The people have "abandoned Me, the fountain of living waters" and followed false gods.

DAY 225

JEREMIAH 4–6

Judah is following false prophets and godless priests. The nation will be punished by an invasion of people who "are cruel and have no mercy."

DAY 226

JEREMIAH 7–9

Jeremiah preaches a message from the temple gate, calling out Judah's horrible practice of child sacrifice, among other sins.

DAY 227

JEREMIAH 10–12

Jeremiah points out that God's people had broken the covenant He gave them at Mount Sinai. "Behold," God says, "I will bring evil on them."

DAY 228

JEREMIAH 13–15

Jeremiah preaches about a terrible drought in Judah. It will be followed by an enemy invasion and the exile of many people.

DAY 229

JEREMIAH 16–19

God tells Jeremiah that he should not marry—his singleness will stand for Judah's separation from God. At a potter's house, Jeremiah learns that God fashions His people like clay.

DAY 230

JEREMIAH 20–22

For his negative prophecies, Jeremiah is punished by other religious leaders. Jeremiah tells Zedekiah, Judah's last king, that he will fall into the Babylonians' hands.

DAY 231

JEREMIAH 23–25

Jeremiah describes a "Branch" from King David's line, a future king who will "execute judgment and justice in the earth." In the near term, Judah faces seventy years of captivity.

DAY 232

JEREMIAH 26–28

Jeremiah wears a yoke to tell King Zedekiah and Judah to "bring your necks under the yoke of the king of Babylon, and serve him and his people, and live."

DAY 233

JEREMIAH 29–30

From Jerusalem, Jeremiah writes to Jewish leaders carried off to Babylon. They must seek the well-being of their new home, "for in its peace you shall have peace."

DAY 234

JEREMIAH 31–32

Though the Babylonians are in control of Judah, God tells Jeremiah to purchase a field. It is a sign that "houses and fields and vineyards shall be possessed again in this land."

DAY 235

JEREMIAH 33–35

Jeremiah again prophesies of a future "Branch" of David who will rule righteously. In the near term, Jerusalem will fall to Babylon and King Zedekiah will be captured.

DAY 236

JEREMIAH 36–38

With Jerusalem under siege, Jeremiah is falsely accused and imprisoned. He urges the king to cooperate with the Babylonians, to limit damage to the city.

DAY 237

JEREMIAH 39–41

The Babylonians break through Jerusalem's walls, destroy the city, and carry its people into captivity. Jeremiah is allowed to stay and serve the Jews left behind.

DAY 238

JEREMIAH 42–44

With the Babylonian-appointed governor of Judah assassinated, several leaders reject Jeremiah's advice and to flee to Egypt. They force Jeremiah to join them.

DAY 239

JEREMIAH 45–47

Earlier prophecies against godless nations are repeated, including one of the Babylonian king Nebuchadnezzar defeating Egypt's Pharaoh Necho in battle.

DAY 240

JEREMIAH 48–49

Prophecies of judgment against Moab, Ammon, Edom, and Damascus are recorded.

DAY 241

JEREMIAH 50

Babylon, which overran Judah and Jerusalem, will soon be conquered—and "all who plunder her shall be satisfied."

DAY 242

JEREMIAH 51–52

Judah's King Zedekiah rebels against the invaders, bringing trouble on Jerusalem. The temple is destroyed, and thousands of important citizens are carried away into exile.

KNOW YOUR BIBLE MEN

DAVID

BOY WONDER

How many are your works, LORD! In wisdom you made them all; the earth is full of your creatures.
PSALM 104:24 NIV

†

Long before David was king of Israel, he was a teenager working the family farm. As a shepherd, David spent countless hours outside. He roamed the plains, hiked the foothills, and slept under the stars. Awestruck by creation, David would write several psalms that share his sense of wonder about the outdoors (see Psalms 8, 19, 29, 65, 104, and 139).

Do you ever feel wonder about creation? A sense of wonder is more than just curiosity. It means you're astonished, amazed, even excited by what you see. When was the last time you let the beauty of the natural world lead you to that place?

Our phones and devices make it easy to ignore what's happening outside. There's always a new text, video, or link to click on. Who cares about which types of clouds are floating by or which phase the moon is in tonight? Why not you? The outside world has much to teach us.

David wrote, "The heavens declare the glory of God; the skies proclaim the work of his hands" (Psalm 19:1 NIV). Feeling wonder about creation will give you a greater understanding of God's character and wisdom (Psalm 19:1–11). Being awestruck by creation will also help you understand your place in the world. God made humankind the caretakers of all that He made (Psalm 8:3–8).

Be like David—let yourself be wowed by nature. Get lost in the wonder of creation, and you will grow closer to God.

Dear God, this natural world is beautiful. I thank You for creating all that You have. Please draw closer to me as I enjoy the world You made.

LAMENTATIONS

AUTHOR

Not stated but traditionally attributed to Jeremiah.

DATE

Probably around 586 BC, shortly after the fall of Jerusalem to the Babylonians.

IN TEN WORDS OR LESS

A despairing poem about the destruction of Jerusalem.

DETAILS, PLEASE

After warning the southern Jewish nation to obey God, the prophet Jeremiah witnesses the punishment he'd threatened. Judah's "enemies prosper, for the LORD has afflicted her because of the multitude of her transgressions," writes Jeremiah. "Her children have gone into captivity before the enemy" (1:5). The sight brings tears to Jeremiah's eyes ("My eye runs down with water," 1:16) and provides his nickname, "the weeping prophet." Lamentations ends with a plaintive cry: "You have utterly rejected us. You are very angry with us" (5:22).

QUOTABLE

- It is because of the LORD's mercies that we are not consumed, because His compassions do not fail. They are new every morning. Great is Your faithfulness. (3:22–23)
- Turn us to You, O LORD, and we shall be restored. Renew our days as of old. (5:21)

UNIQUE AND UNUSUAL

Though Lamentations doesn't indicate its author, Jeremiah is described in 2 Chronicles as a composer of laments (35:25).

SO WHAT?

God's punishment might seem severe, but as the book of Hebrews says, "No chastening seems to be joyous for the present, but grievous; nevertheless, afterward it yields the peaceful fruit of righteousness to those who are exercised by it" (12:11).

DAY 243

LAMENTATIONS 1–2

Sad poems mourn the destruction of Jerusalem by the Babylonians. "Jerusalem has grievously sinned," the writer says. "Therefore she has been removed."

DAY 244

LAMENTATIONS 3–5

In his terrible sorrow, Lamentations' author—perhaps Jeremiah—recognizes that "it is because of the LORD's mercies that we are not consumed, because His compassions do not fail."

EZEKIEL

AUTHOR

Ezekiel, a priest (1:1–3).

DATE

Approximately the 590s–570s BC.

IN TEN WORDS OR LESS

Though Israel is in exile, the nation will be restored.

DETAILS, PLEASE

Ezekiel, an exiled Jew in Babylon, becomes God's spokesman to fellow exiles. He shares unusual (even bizarre) visions with the people, reminding them of the sin that led to their captivity but also offering hope of national restoration.

QUOTABLE

- "I have no pleasure in the death of him who dies," says the Lord God. "Therefore, turn yourselves and live." (18:32)

UNIQUE AND UNUSUAL

Ezekiel's vision of a valley of dry bones is one of the Bible's strangest images: "I prophesied as I was commanded, and. . .there was a noise, and behold, a shaking, and the bones came together. . . . The sinews and the flesh came up on them, and the skin covered them above. . . . And the breath came into them, and they lived and stood up on their feet, an exceedingly great army" (37:7–8, 10).

SO WHAT?

Ezekiel strongly teaches personal responsibility: "The soul that sins, it shall die. But if a man is just and does what is lawful and right. . .he shall surely live" (18:4–5, 9).

DAY 245

EZEKIEL 1–3

Ezekiel, a Jewish priest in Babylon, is called to be prophet to his fellow exiles. God calls Ezekiel "son of man," and sends him to a "hardhearted" people.

DAY 246

EZEKIEL 4–7

Ezekiel acts out messages for the people. By dividing his own hair into thirds, then burning, chopping, and scattering each part, he shows the punishment coming on Jerusalem.

DAY 247

EZEKIEL 8–11

In a vision, Ezekiel sees six angels destroying everyone in Jerusalem except for those who were sad about the city's sin.

DAY 248

EZEKIEL 12–15

Ezekiel continues to act out prophecies. He digs through a wall to leave his own house, a symbol of the coming Babylonian invasion and exile.

DAY 249

EZEKIEL 16–17

Jerusalem cheats on God by chasing false gods and even burning children in sacrifice. But Ezekiel still describes a future time when Israel will again honor God.

DAY 250

EZEKIEL 18–20

Through Ezekiel, God teaches individual responsibility: "The soul that sins, it shall die." And God takes no pleasure in anyone's death: "Turn yourselves and live."

DAY 251

EZEKIEL 21–22

God accuses His people of bloodshed, robbery, and oppressing others: "Therefore I have poured out My indignation on them."

DAY 252

EZEKIEL 23–24

God describes Israel and Judah as two badly behaved sisters. As a sign to the people, Ezekiel is told not to show sadness when his wife dies.

DAY 253

EZEKIEL 25–27

Ezekiel describes God's judgment on the surrounding nations of Ammon, Moab, Edom, Philistia, and Tyre for their many sins.

DAY 254

EZEKIEL 28–30

The king of Tyre is criticized for his pride in language that seems to describe Satan's fall into sin. The future regathering of Israel is again mentioned.

DAY 255

EZEKIEL 31–32

Ezekiel prophesies God's judgment on Egypt and the pharaoh. The Lord will use "the sword of the king of Babylon."

DAY 256

EZEKIEL 33–34

God criticizes Israel's "shepherds" (leaders) for their selfishness and greed. The Lord promises to someday set up "one shepherd over them, even My servant David."

DAY 257

EZEKIEL 35–36

God promises to restore Israel "for My holy name's sake," even though their behavior embarrassed Him before other nations.

DAY 258

EZEKIEL 37–39

Ezekiel has a vision of a valley full of dry bones which are restored to life. It's a symbol of the future restoration of God's people.

DAY 259

EZEKIEL 40–42

Twenty-five years into the captivity, Ezekiel sees a vision of a beautiful future temple of God.

DAY 260

EZEKIEL 43–44

In a vision, Ezekiel sees God's glory filling the temple. God describes His expectations for the priests who serve in the temple.

DAY 261

EZEKIEL 45–46

Ezekiel describes how worship will take place in the future temple.

DAY 262

EZEKIEL 47–48

Ezekiel describes a river coming out of the future temple, feeding many trees on its banks and healing the Dead Sea. The name of the city becomes, "The Lord is there."

KNOW YOUR BIBLE *MEN*

ELIJAH

CONFIDENCE IN GOD

"Answer me, LORD, answer me, so these people will know that you, LORD, are God, and that you are turning their hearts back again."
1 KINGS 18:37 NIV

†

It's easy to lose confidence in people. Parents get too busy, and something falls through the cracks. Suddenly, you're stuck without a ride on an important day. Coaches don't always follow through on what they say they'll do. You never get that extra practice you were promised. Teachers get stressed and snap at the class. Siblings bother us, accidentally or intentionally. Even friends can let us down.

Elijah the prophet was full of confidence—but it wasn't confidence in any other person. Elijah was confident in God. In one of the Bible's epic showdowns, the great prophet challenged a large group of followers of the false god Baal to see whose deity was real. Whichever god's offering was burned up first would prove to be the true one (1 Kings 18:16–24). After watching Baal's followers humiliate themselves as they begged their idol to consume their offering, Elijah actually took the time to soak down his altar with gallons and gallons of water. Then he prayed confidently, and the fire fell. Everything—the sacrifice, the altar, and the water surrounding it—was incinerated (1 Kings 18:25–38).

God will never let you down. People, on the other hand, will. When that happens, show them your kindness and forgiveness and turn your heart to God. As Psalm 27:13–14 (NIV) says, "I remain confident of this: I will see the goodness of the LORD. . .be strong and take heart and wait for the LORD."

Heavenly Father, You are truly powerful and good. You have proven that You are the one true God and that no idol compares. As I place my full confidence in You, please bless and guide me.

DANIEL

AUTHOR

Likely Daniel, though some question this. Chapters 7–12 are written in the first person ("I Daniel," 7:15), though the first six chapters are in the third person ("Then Daniel answered," 2:14).

DATE

The period of the Babylonian captivity, approximately 605–538 BC.

IN TEN WORDS OR LESS

Faithful to God in a challenging setting, Daniel is blessed.

DETAILS, PLEASE

As a young man, Daniel—along with three others to be known as Shadrach, Meshach, and Abednego—are taken from their home in Jerusalem to serve the king of Babylon. Daniel's God-given ability to interpret dreams endears him to King Nebuchadnezzar, whose vision of a huge statue, Daniel says, represents existing and future kingdoms. Shadrach, Meshach, and Abednego find trouble when they disobey an order to bow before a statue of Nebuchadnezzar; as punishment, they are thrown into a fiery furnace, where they are protected by an angelic being "like the Son of God" (3:25). The next Babylonian king, Belshazzar, throws a drinking party using cups stolen from the temple in Jerusalem; he literally sees "the writing on the wall," which Daniel interprets as the soon-to-come takeover of Babylon by the Medes. The Median king, Darius, keeps Daniel as an adviser but is tricked into passing a law designed by other jealous officials to hurt Daniel, who ends up in a den of lions. Once again, God protects His people; Daniel spends a night before being replaced by the schemers, who are mauled by the hungry beasts. The final six chapters contain Daniel's prophetic visions, including that of "seventy weeks" of the end times.

QUOTABLE

- "Our God whom we serve is able to deliver us from the burning fiery furnace. And He will deliver us out of your hand, O king." (3:17)
- "My God has sent His angel and has shut the lions' mouths, that they have not hurt me." (6:22)
- "O my God. . .we do not present our supplications before You because of our righteous acts, but because of Your great mercies." (9:18)

UNIQUE AND UNUSUAL

The book was originally written in two languages: Hebrew (the introduction and most of the prophecies, chapter 1 and chapters 8–12) and Aramaic (the stories of chapters 2–7).

SO WHAT?

As the old song says, "Dare to be a Daniel." God will always take care of the people who "dare to stand alone. . .to have a purpose firm" for Him.

DAY 263

DANIEL 1–2

Daniel and three friends are among bright young Jews taken to serve in conquering Babylon. He interprets the king's dreams and is promoted to leadership.

DAY 264

DANIEL 3–4

Babylon's king, Nebuchadnezzar, orders all people to worship a golden statue. Daniel's three friends refuse and are thrown into a burning furnace. God rescues them.

DAY 265

DANIEL 5–6

Daniel reads the handwriting on the wall for King Belshazzar. Under the Persian king Darius, Daniel is thrown into a den of lions for praying to God. The Lord rescues Daniel.

DAY 266

DANIEL 7–9

Daniel has visions of coming world kingdoms, the end times, and "the Son of man" coming in the clouds, who will rule with "everlasting dominion."

DAY 267

DANIEL 10–12

Daniel tells of the end-times events. A terrible "time of trouble" will be followed by the resurrection of people, "some to everlasting life and some to shame and everlasting contempt."

HOSEA

AUTHOR

Probably Hosea himself, though the text is in both the first and the third person.

DATE

Sometime between 750 (approximately when Hosea began ministering) and 722 BC (when Assyria overran Israel).

IN TEN WORDS OR LESS

Prophet's marriage to prostitute reflects God's relationship with Israel.

DETAILS, PLEASE

God gives Hosea a strange command: "Take for yourself a wife of prostitution" (1:2). The marriage pictures God's relationship to Israel—an honorable, loving husband paired with an unfaithful wife. Hosea marries an adulteress named Gomer and starts a family with her. When Gomer returns to her life of sin, Hosea—again picturing God's faithfulness—buys her back from the slave market. The book contains God's warnings for disobedience but also His promises of blessing for repentance.

QUOTABLE

- "For they [Israel] have sown the wind, and they shall reap the whirlwind." (8:7)

UNIQUE AND UNUSUAL

Gomer had three children—perhaps Hosea's but maybe not—each given a prophetic name. Son Jezreel was named for a massacre, daughter Lo-ruhamah's name meant "not loved," and son Lo-ammi's name meant "not my people."

SO WHAT?

God is faithful, even when His people aren't—and He's always ready to forgive. "I will heal their backsliding," God said through Hosea; "I will love them freely" (14:4).

DAY 268

HOSEA 1–5

God tells Hosea to take a wife who will be unfaithful to him. This stands for God's relationship with Israel. Then Hosea is to pursue his straying wife as God pursues His people.

DAY 269

HOSEA 6–10

God calls out the northern kingdom's sin and trust in other nations rather than Him. "You have plowed wickedness," He tells Israel. "You have reaped iniquity."

DAY 270

HOSEA 11–14

Israel will come under control of the vicious Assyrians. But God will one day "heal their backsliding" and "love them freely."

JOEL

AUTHOR

Joel, son of Pethuel (1:1). Little else is known about him.

DATE

Unclear but possibly just before the Babylonian invasion of Judah in 586 BC.

IN TEN WORDS OR LESS

Locust plague pictures God's judgment on His sinful people.

DETAILS, PLEASE

A devastating locust swarm invades the nation of Judah, but Joel indicates this natural disaster is nothing compared to the coming "great and very terrible" day of the Lord (2:11). God plans to judge His people for sin, but they still have time to repent. Obedience will bring both physical and spiritual renewal: "I will pour out My Spirit on all flesh," God says (2:28). When the Holy Spirit comes on Christian believers at Pentecost, the apostle Peter quotes this passage to explain what has happened (Acts 2:17).

QUOTABLE

- And tear your heart and not your garments, and turn to the LORD your God, for He is gracious and merciful, slow to anger and of great kindness, and relents from doing evil. (2:13)
- Whoever calls on the name of the LORD shall be delivered. (2:32)
- Multitudes, multitudes in the valley of decision, for the day of the LORD is near in the valley of decision. (3:14)
- The LORD also shall roar out of Zion and utter His voice from Jerusalem. And the heavens and the earth shall shake. But the LORD will be the hope of His people and the strength of the children of Israel. (3:16)

UNIQUE AND UNUSUAL

Unlike other prophets who condemned idolatry, injustice, or other specific sins of the Jewish people, Joel simply called for repentance without describing the sin committed.

SO WHAT?

Though God judges sin, He always offers a way out—in our time, through Jesus.

DAY 271

JOEL 1–3

Insects are ruining the land. Joel uses this disaster as a picture of God's coming judgment for His people's sin. But one day He will "pour out [His] Spirit on all flesh."

AMOS

AUTHOR

Amos, a shepherd from Tekoa, near Bethlehem (1:1).

DATE

Approximately the 760s BC.

IN TEN WORDS OR LESS

Real religion isn't just ritual but treating people with justice.

DETAILS, PLEASE

An average guy—a lowly shepherd, actually—takes on the rich and powerful of Israelite society, condemning their idol worship, persecution of God's prophets, and cheating of the poor. Though God once rescued the people of Israel from slavery in Egypt, He is ready to send them into new bondage because of their sin. Amos sees visions that picture Israel's plight: a plumb line, indicating the people are not measuring up to God's standards, and a basket of ripe fruit, showing the nation is ripe for God's judgment.

QUOTABLE

- "Prepare to meet your God, O Israel!" (4:12)
- Seek good, and not evil, that you may live. (5:14)
- "Let judgment run down like waters and righteousness like a mighty stream." (5:24)
- Then Amos answered and said to Amaziah, "I was no prophet, nor was I a prophet's son. But I was a herdsman and a gatherer of sycamore fruit." (7:14)

UNIQUE AND UNUSUAL

A native of the southern Jewish kingdom of Judah, Amos was directed by God to prophesy in the northern Jewish nation of Israel.

SO WHAT?

How are you treating the people around you? In God's eyes, that's an indicator of your true spiritual condition. For a New Testament perspective, see James 2:14–18.

DAY 272

AMOS 1-5

God calls a shepherd to be prophet to Israel and Judah in their times of success. Amos criticizes them, among other things, for mistreating the poor.

DAY 273

AMOS 6-9; OBADIAH

Amos warns God's people that they will be carried off by enemies. Obadiah describes doom for the enemy nation of Edom; "But on Mount Zion shall be deliverance."

OBADIAH

AUTHOR

Obadiah (verse 1), perhaps a person by that name or an unnamed prophet for whom "Obadiah" (meaning "servant of God") is a title.

DATE

Unclear but probably within thirty years after Babylon's invasion of Judah in 586 BC.

IN TEN WORDS OR LESS

Edom will suffer for participating in Jerusalem's destruction.

DETAILS, PLEASE

Edom was a nation descended from Esau—twin brother of Jacob, the patriarch of Israel. The baby boys had struggled in their mother's womb (Genesis 25:21–26), and their conflict had continued over the centuries. After Edom took part in the Babylonian ransacking of Jerusalem, Obadiah passed down God's judgment: "For your violence against your brother Jacob, shame shall cover you, and you shall be cut off forever" (verse 10).

QUOTABLE

- "On Mount Zion shall be deliverance." (verse 17)

UNIQUE AND UNUSUAL

Obadiah is the Old Testament's shortest book—only one chapter and 21 verses.

SO WHAT?

Obadiah shows God's faithfulness to His people. This prophecy is a fulfillment of God's promise from generations earlier: "I will bless those who bless you and curse him who curses you" (Genesis 12:3).

JONAH

AUTHOR

Unclear; the story is Jonah's but is written in the third person.

DATE

Approximately 760 BC. Jonah prophesied during the reign of Israel's King Jeroboam II (see 2 Kings 14:23–25), who ruled from about 793 to 753 BC.

IN TEN WORDS OR LESS

Reluctant prophet, running from God, is swallowed by giant fish.

DETAILS, PLEASE

God tells Jonah to preach repentance in Nineveh, capital of the brutal Assyrian Empire. Jonah disobeys, sailing in the opposite direction—toward a rendezvous with literary immortality. A storm rocks Jonah's ship, and he spends three days in a giant fish's belly before deciding to obey God after all. When Jonah preaches, Nineveh repents—and God spares the city from the destruction He'd threatened. But the prejudiced Jonah pouts. The story ends with God proclaiming his concern even for vicious pagans.

QUOTABLE

- And he said to them, "I am a Hebrew, and I fear the LORD, the God of heaven, who has made the sea and the dry land." (1:9)
- I will pay what I have vowed. Salvation is of the LORD. (2:9)
- And God saw their works—that they turned from their evil way—and God relented of the disaster that He had said that He would do to them. And He did not do it. (3:10)
- "Should not I spare Nineveh, that great city, in which are more than one hundred and twenty thousand persons who cannot discern between their right hand and their left hand?" (4:11)

UNIQUE AND UNUSUAL

Jonah's prophecy didn't come true—because of Nineveh's repentance.

SO WHAT?

God loves everyone—even the enemies of His chosen people. As Romans 5:8 says, "God demonstrates His love toward us, in that while we were still sinners, Christ died for us."

DAY 274

JONAH 1–4

A reluctant prophet tries to avoid preaching to the wicked city of Nineveh. God gets Jonah's attention in a miraculous way. He obeys, and the godless people repent.

KNOW YOUR BIBLE *MEN*

DANIEL

THE OTHER, THE OUTSIDER

Among those who were chosen were some from Judah:
Daniel, Hananiah, Mishael and Azariah.
Daniel 1:6 NIV

†

Everything about Daniel made him different. His name. His ethnicity. His religion. Daniel was also a standout young man, talented and handsome. But he was a Jew in Babylon. Daniel was one of the conquered and captured people. The Jews were second-class citizens and completely other. The book of Daniel tells his story of rising in the ranks of Babylonian culture, eventually to a place of leadership (Daniel 2:48). He never wavered from his commitment to God. Through Daniel's story, we see how God will use faithful followers to influence others—sometimes in an unexpected place like the royal court of Babylon. We also see that God is personal (Daniel 3:24–25) and that He saves (Daniel 6:22), two qualities Jesus would exemplify years after Daniel's time.

Perhaps the most striking thing about Daniel's story is that it shows how "others" can make a difference. Life is full of times when you'll feel like an outsider. You won't make the team. You won't be invited to hang out with a certain group. You won't make as much money as some people you know. You won't look the same, sound the same, or believe the same as those around you. But you don't have to be part of the majority. You are never an outsider to God—you're His child (1 John 3:1). As He did with Daniel, God will use your faithfulness to influence others for good.

Thank You, God, for loving outsiders. Thank You for honoring faithfulness. Help me to be faithful to You in every circumstance. Whether I'm on the outside or the inside, help me always to remember that You are my heavenly Father.

MICAH

AUTHOR

"The word of the Lord that came to Micah of Moresheth" (1:1). Micah either wrote the prophecies or dictated them to another.

DATE

Approximately 700 BC.

IN TEN WORDS OR LESS

Israel and Judah will suffer for their idolatry and injustice.

DETAILS, PLEASE

Micah chastises both the northern and southern Jewish nations for pursuing false gods and cheating the poor. The two nations will be devastated by invaders (the Assyrians), but God will preserve "the remnant of Israel" (2:12).

QUOTABLE

- And many nations shall come and say, "Come, let us go up to the mountain of the Lord and to the house of the God of Jacob, and He will teach us of His ways, and we will walk in His paths." For the law shall go forth from Zion, and the word of the Lord from Jerusalem. (4:2)
- He has shown you, O man, what is good. And what does the Lord require of you, but to act justly and to love mercy and to walk humbly with your God? (6:8)

UNIQUE AND UNUSUAL

Centuries before Jesus' birth, Micah predicted the town where it would occur: "But you, Bethlehem Ephrathah, though you are little among the thousands of Judah, yet out of you shall come forth to Me He who is to be ruler in Israel" (5:2).

SO WHAT?

Micah shows how God's judgment is tempered by mercy. "Who is a God like You, who pardons guilt and passes by the transgression of the remnant of His heritage? He does not retain His anger forever, because He delights in mercy" (7:18).

DAY 275

MICAH 1–7

Micah prophesies trouble for God's sinful people in the northern kingdom of Israel. But he also predicts the exact birthplace of the coming Messiah: Bethlehem in Judah.

NAHUM

AUTHOR

"The book of the vision of Nahum the Elkoshite" (1:1). Nahum either wrote the prophecies or dictated them to another.

DATE

Sometime between 663 and 612 BC.

IN TEN WORDS OR LESS

Powerful, wicked Nineveh will fall before God's judgment.

DETAILS, PLEASE

"Woe to the bloody city!" Nahum cries (3:1). Nineveh, capital of the brutal Assyrian Empire, has been targeted for judgment by God Himself, who will "make you vile, and will set you as a spectacle" (3:6) for sins of idolatry and cruelty. Nahum's prophecy comes true when the Babylonian Empire overruns Nineveh in 612 BC.

QUOTABLE

- The LORD is slow to anger and great in power and will not at all acquit the wicked. (1:3)
- The LORD is good, a stronghold in the day of trouble, and He knows those who trust in Him. (1:7)
- Woe to the bloody city! It is all full of lies and robbery; the prey does not depart. (3:1)

UNIQUE AND UNUSUAL

Nahum is a kind of Jonah, part 2. Though the city had once avoided God's judgment by taking Jonah's preaching to heart and repenting, now, more than a century later, it will experience the full consequence of its sins.

SO WHAT?

Even the most powerful city on earth is no match for God's strength. Neither is the biggest problem in our individual lives.

DAY 276

NAHUM 1–3; HABAKKUK 1–3

Nahum speaks doom on the "bloody city" of Nineveh, capital of Assyria. Habakkuk asks how God can use "bitter and hasty" Chaldeans (Babylonians) in His plans.

HABAKKUK

AUTHOR

Habakkuk (1:1); nothing is known of his background.

DATE

Approximately 600 BC.

IN TEN WORDS OR LESS

Trust God even when He seems unresponsive or unfair.

DETAILS, PLEASE

In Judah, a prophet complains that God allows violence and injustice among His people. But Habakkuk is shocked to learn the Lord's plan for dealing with the problem: sending the "bitter and hasty" (1:6) Chaldeans to punish Judah. Habakkuk argues that the Chaldeans are far worse than the disobedient Jews, telling God, "You are of purer eyes than to behold evil and cannot look at iniquity" (1:13). The Lord, however, says He's only using the Chaldeans for His purposes and will in time punish them for their own sins. It's not Habakkuk's job to question God's ways: "The Lord is in His holy temple. Let all the earth keep silence before Him" (2:20). Habakkuk, like Job, ultimately submits to God's authority.

QUOTABLE

- "The just shall live by his faith." (2:4)
- "What profit is the carved image that its maker has carved it, the cast metal image, and a teacher of lies, that the maker of his work trusts in it, to make mute idols?" (2:18)
- "Although the fig tree shall not blossom, nor shall fruit be on the vines, the labor of the olive shall fail, and the fields shall yield no food, the flock shall be cut off from the fold, and there shall be no herd in the stalls, yet I will rejoice in the Lord. I will rejoice in the God of my salvation." (3:17–18)

UNIQUE AND UNUSUAL

The apostle Paul quotes Habakkuk 2:4 in his powerful gospel presentation in Romans 1.

SO WHAT?

Our world is much like Habakkuk's—full of violence and injustice—but God is still in control. Whether we sense it or not, He's working out His own purposes.

KNOW YOUR BIBLE *MEN*

MORDECAI

WISE AND BRAVE

"Who knows but that you have come to your
royal position for such a time as this?"
ESTHER 4:14 NIV

†

In movies about Esther, Mordecai is a supporting character. The story is primarily about the beautiful young queen, a plot against her people, and the decision to risk her life for them. But let's take a minute to focus on Mordecai. There's more to him than you might at first realize.

Mordecai was a multi-faceted man. He was an adoptive father (2:7), something of a spy (2:21–23), a committed follower of God (5:9), and a government official (8:2). Most importantly, Mordecai is someone who spoke up at the right time. The turning point in Esther's story is her conversation with Mordecai. After discovering a plot to commit genocide against the Jews, Mordecai asked Esther to consider if maybe God made her queen for a reason (4:13–14). Mordecai was wise enough to understand what God was doing and brave enough to speak up, even though he was risking his life.

Growing in wisdom—and knowing when to speak up—is part of becoming a Christian man. The Bible is full of instruction on when to speak and listen, and how to use your words (Proverbs 18:21; 21:23; James 3:1–12). As you grow into manhood, consider Mordecai. He didn't become a wise supporting character by accident. As a faithful follower of God, he had learned these truths and how to apply them. Now, as God did with Mordecai, He may just use you at the turning point of someone's very important story.

Thank You, God, for Your wise instruction about the use of my words. Help me to grow into a wise man. Please show me when it's best to speak up and use me for Your good purposes.

ZEPHANIAH

AUTHOR

Zephaniah (1:1).

DATE

Approximately 640–620 BC, during the reign of King Josiah (1:1).

IN TEN WORDS OR LESS

A coming "day of the LORD" promises heavy judgment.

DETAILS, PLEASE

Zephaniah begins with a jarring prophecy: "I will utterly destroy all things from off the land," God declares in the book's second verse. People, animals, birds, and fish will all perish, victims of God's wrath over Judah's idolatry. Other nearby nations will be punished, as well, in "the fire of My jealousy" (3:8), but there is hope: In His mercy, God will one day restore a remnant of Israel that "shall not do iniquity or speak lies" (3:13).

QUOTABLE

- The great day of the Lord is near; it is near and hastens greatly, even the sound of the day of the Lord. (1:14)
- Neither their silver nor their gold shall be able to deliver them on the day of the Lord's wrath, but the whole land shall be devoured by the fire of His jealousy. (1:18)
- Seek the Lord, all you meek of the earth, who have worked His justice; seek righteousness, seek humility. It may be you shall be hidden on the day of the Lord's anger. (2:3)
- The Lord your God in your midst is mighty. He will save; He will rejoice over you with joy. (3:17)

UNIQUE AND UNUSUAL

Zephaniah gives more detail about himself than most of the minor prophets, identifying himself as a great-great-grandson of Hezekiah (1:1), probably the popular, godly king of Judah (2 Chronicles 29).

SO WHAT?

God gave the people of Judah fair warning of His judgment, just as He has done with us. For Christians, the coming "day of the LORD" carries no fear.

DAY 277

ZEPHANIAH 1–3; HAGGAI 1–2

Zephaniah warns sinful Jerusalem of judgment but promises a future blessing. Haggai demands that the Jews coming back from exile finish their work on God's temple.

HAGGAI

AUTHOR

Haggai (1:1).

DATE

520 BC—a precise date because Haggai mentions "the second year of Darius the king" (1:1), which can be verified against Persian records.

IN TEN WORDS OR LESS

Jews returning from exile need to rebuild God's temple.

DETAILS, PLEASE

One of three "postexilic" prophets, Haggai encourages former Babylonian captives to restore the demolished temple in Jerusalem. The new world power, Persia, has allowed the people to return to Jerusalem, but they've become distracted with building their own comfortable homes. Through Haggai, God tells the people to rebuild the temple first in order to break a drought that's affecting the countryside.

QUOTABLE

- "'Be strong, all you people of the land,' says the Lord, 'and work. For I am with you,' says the Lord of hosts." (2:4)

UNIQUE AND UNUSUAL

Haggai seems to hint at the end-times tribulation and second coming of Christ when he quotes God as saying, "I will shake the heavens and the earth and the sea and the dry land. And I will shake all nations, and the desire of all nations shall come" (2:6–7).

SO WHAT?

Priorities are important. When we put God first, He is more inclined to bless us.

ZECHARIAH

AUTHOR

Zechariah, son of Berechiah (1:1); some believe a second, unnamed writer contributed chapters 9–14.

DATE

Approximately 520–475 BC.

IN TEN WORDS OR LESS

Jewish exiles should rebuild their temple—and anticipate their Messiah.

DETAILS, PLEASE

Like Haggai, another postexilic prophet, Zechariah urges Jewish people to rebuild the Jerusalem temple. He also gives several prophecies of the coming Messiah, including an end-times vision of a final battle over Jerusalem, when "the Lord shall go forth and fight against those nations. . . . His feet shall stand on the Mount of Olives. . . . And the Lord shall be King over all the earth" (14:3–4, 9).

QUOTABLE

- "'Turn to Me,' says the Lord of hosts, 'and I will turn to you.'" (1:3)

UNIQUE AND UNUSUAL

Zechariah's prophecy of the Messiah riding a donkey into Jerusalem (9:9) was fulfilled to the letter in Jesus' "triumphal entry" (Matthew 21:1–11). The prophecy, "They shall look on Me whom they have pierced" (12:10), refers to the Roman soldiers' spearing of Christ after the crucifixion (John 19:34).

SO WHAT?

Knowing that many of Zechariah's specific prophecies were fulfilled in Jesus, we can trust that his other predictions—of the end times—will come true too.

DAY 278

ZECHARIAH 1–4

A prophet and priest after the exile, Zechariah describes a day when God will come and dwell in the midst of His people.

DAY 279

ZECHARIAH 5–9

Zechariah's prophecies include one of a King entering Jerusalem "lowly, and riding on a donkey, and on a colt, the foal of a donkey."

DAY 280

ZECHARIAH 10–14

In an end-times battle, God "will gather all nations against Jerusalem." But this will be followed by a day when "the Lord shall be King over all the earth."

MALACHI

AUTHOR

Malachi (1:1), meaning "my messenger." No other details are given.

DATE

Approximately 450 BC.

IN TEN WORDS OR LESS

The Jews have become careless in their attitude toward God.

DETAILS, PLEASE

Prophesying a century after the return from exile, Malachi chastises the Jews for offering "lame and sick" sacrifices (1:8); for divorcing their wives to marry pagan women (2:11, 14); and for failing to pay tithes for the temple (3:8). The Lord was angry with the attitude "It is vain to serve God" (3:14), but He promised to bless the obedient: "To you who fear My name, the Sun of righteousness shall arise with healing in His wings" (4:2).

QUOTABLE

- "I have loved you," says the Lord. "Yet you say, 'In what way have You loved us?' Was not Esau Jacob's brother?" says the Lord, "yet I loved Jacob, and I hated Esau and laid his mountains and his heritage waste for the jackals of the wilderness." (1:2–3)
- Do we not all have one Father? Has not one God created us? Why do we act treacherously, every man against his brother, by profaning the covenant of our fathers? (2:10)
- "Return to Me, and I will return to you," says the Lord of hosts. (3:7)

UNIQUE AND UNUSUAL

Malachi, the last book of the Old Testament, contains the final word from God for some four hundred years, until the appearance of John the Baptist and Jesus, the Messiah, as prophesied in Malachi 3:1: "I will send My messenger, and he shall prepare the way before Me. And the Lord, whom you seek, shall suddenly come to His temple."

SO WHAT?

God doesn't want empty religious rituals—He wants people to worship Him "in spirit and in truth" (John 4:24).

DAY 281

MALACHI 1–4

Malachi urges the returned exiles to do their duty before God. In the distant future, "the Sun of righteousness shall arise with healing in His wings."

MATTHEW

AUTHOR

Not stated but traditionally attributed to Matthew, a tax collector (9:9). Matthew is also known as "Levi" (Mark 2:14).

DATE

Approximately AD 70, when Romans destroyed the temple in Jerusalem.

IN TEN WORDS OR LESS

Jesus fulfills the Old Testament prophecies of a coming Messiah.

DETAILS, PLEASE

The first of the four Gospels (meaning "good news"), the book of Matthew ties what follows in the New Testament to what came before in the Old. The book, written primarily to a Jewish audience, uses numerous Old Testament references to prove that Jesus is the promised Messiah the Jews have been anticipating for centuries. Beginning with a genealogy that shows Jesus' ancestry through King David and the patriarch Abraham, Matthew then details the angelic announcement of Jesus' conception and the visit of the "wise men" with their gifts of gold, frankincense, and myrrh. Matthew introduces the character of John the Baptist, relative and forerunner of Jesus, and describes the calling of key disciples Peter, Andrew, James, and John. Jesus' teachings are emphasized, with long passages covering His Sermon on the Mount (chapters 5–7), including the Beatitudes ("Blessed are the. . .") and the Lord's Prayer ("Our Father who is in heaven. . ."). As with all four Gospels, Matthew also details the death, burial, and resurrection of Jesus and is the only biographer of Jesus to mention several miracles—an earthquake, the breaking open of tombs, and the raising to life of dead saints—that occurred during that time (27:50–54).

QUOTABLE

- "She shall bring forth a Son, and you shall call His name JESUS, for He shall save His people from their sins." (1:21)

- "You are the salt of the earth. . . . You are the light of the world." (5:13–14)
- "Love your enemies, bless those who curse you, do good to those who hate you, and pray for those who despitefully use you and persecute you." (5:44)
- "Do not judge, that you not be judged." (7:1)
- "Ask, and it shall be given to you. Seek, and you shall find. Knock, and it shall be opened to you." (7:7)
- "Therefore go and teach all nations, baptizing them in the name of the Father and of the Son and of the Holy Spirit." (28:19)

UNIQUE AND UNUSUAL

Matthew is the only Gospel to use the terms "church" and "kingdom of heaven."

SO WHAT?

As Messiah, Jesus is also King—and worthy of our worship.

DAY 282

MATTHEW 1-4

Jesus is born in the family line of David, baptized by His relative John, and tempted by Satan. He calls disciples and begins His ministry in Capernaum of Galilee.

DAY 283

MATTHEW 5-7

In the Sermon on the Mount, Jesus says He did not come "to destroy the Law or the Prophets," but to fulfill them.

DAY 284

MATTHEW 8–9

Jesus proves His power by healing diseases, casting out demons, controlling the weather, and raising the dead. He calls the tax collector Matthew as a disciple.

DAY 285

MATTHEW 10–11

Jesus' twelve disciples are sent out to preach to "the lost sheep of the house of Israel." He offers rest to those "who labor and are heavy-laden."

DAY 286

MATTHEW 12–13

Jesus calls Himself "Lord even of the Sabbath day." He hints of His coming death and resurrection and teaches of the kingdom of heaven in parables.

DAY 287

MATTHEW 14–16

Jesus miraculously feeds crowds of four and five thousand people. He increases His criticism of the Jewish religious leaders, the scribes and Pharisees.

DAY 288

MATTHEW 17–19

The disciples Peter, James, and John see Jesus' true glory during His transfiguration. Jesus speaks plainly of His coming death and resurrection.

DAY 289

MATTHEW 20–21

Jesus explains His coming crucifixion and resurrection. He tells Jewish leaders, "The kingdom of God shall be taken from you and given to a nation bringing forth its fruits."

DAY 290

MATTHEW 22–23

Jesus quiets the Pharisees with His questions. Then He explains why they're in trouble: "For you shut up the kingdom of heaven against men."

DAY 291

MATTHEW 24–25

In His Olivet Discourse, Jesus describes the bad condition of the world before His second coming. In the end, He will separate the good from the wicked.

DAY 292

MATTHEW 26

Judas Iscariot agrees to betray Jesus to Jewish leaders. Jesus has His last supper with the disciples, then prays at Gethsemane. He is arrested, and His disciples run away.

DAY 293

MATTHEW 27–28

Jesus is falsely accused, mocked, crucified, and buried. On the third day, angels announce, "He has risen." Jesus tells His followers to "teach all nations" about Him.

KNOW YOUR BIBLE MEN

JOSEPH

GOD IS WITH YOU

Then Joseph, being raised from sleep, did as the angel of the Lord had told him and took to him his wife, and did not know her until she had brought forth her firstborn Son. And he called His name Jesus.
Matthew 1:24–25

†

It must have required enormous faith for Joseph to understand what the angel said. . .then obey his commands. Joseph's fiancée Mary was pregnant, yet still a virgin. How is that possible? The baby would "save His people from their sins" (Matthew 1:21). What could that mean? Joseph, as a faithful Jew, surely knew God's laws for atonement and forgiveness. Was this baby really going to change hundreds of years of Jewish tradition? Joseph's head was probably spinning with questions.

But Joseph trusted God's plan and refrained from having sex with his new wife (Matthew 1:25). Most men have a tough time mastering their sexual urges. It couldn't have been easy for Joseph, either—he was a regular guy! He may have felt confused or disappointed about this strange start to his married life. Sometimes, living out your faith is difficult.

But no matter how challenging it was, Joseph was willing to wait for God's plan to unfold. He put everything on hold—even sex with his wife—and trusted God's timing.

Do you think Joseph could be a role model for you? Why not resolve to master your sexual urges and wait on God's timing too? Some days, that may seem impossible. But as the angel told Joseph, Jesus is "Immanuel" —meaning He is with you, even in the waiting.

Dear God, I know that my body is a gift from You. So, I pray for Your help to master my sexual urges. Please help me to wait for Your timing. Thank You, Jesus, for being "God with us."

MARK

AUTHOR

Not stated but traditionally attributed to John Mark, a missionary companion of Paul and Barnabas (Acts 12:25) and an associate of the apostle Peter (1 Peter 5:13).

DATE

Probably AD 60s, during the Roman persecution of Christians.

IN TEN WORDS OR LESS

Jesus is God's Son, a suffering servant of all people.

DETAILS, PLEASE

The second of the four Gospels is believed by most to be the first one written. The book of Mark is the briefest and most active of the four biographies of Jesus, the majority of which is repeated in the Gospels of Matthew and Luke. Mark addresses a Gentile audience, portraying Jesus as a man of action, divinely capable of healing the sick, controlling nature, and battling the powers of Satan. Mark's theme of the suffering servant comes through in his narratives of Jesus' interaction with hostile doubters—the Jewish leaders, who want to kill Him (9:31); His neighbors, who take offense at Him (6:3); and even His own family members, who think He's crazy (3:21). The abasement of Jesus pictures what His disciples should pursue: "Whoever wants to be great among you shall be your minister, and whoever of you wants to be the first shall be servant of all. For even the Son of Man came not to be ministered to, but to minister, and to give His life as a ransom for many" (10:43–45).

QUOTABLE

- "Come after Me, and I will make you to become fishers of men." (1:17)
- "Allow the little children to come to Me, and do not forbid them, for of such is the kingdom of God." (10:14)

- "It is easier for a camel to go through the eye of a needle than for a rich man to enter into the kingdom of God." (10:25)
- "Render to Caesar the things that are Caesar's, and to God the things that are God's." (12:17)
- "Watch and pray, lest you enter into temptation. The spirit truly is willing, but the body is weak." (14:38)

UNIQUE AND UNUSUAL

Many believe an unnamed spectator at Jesus' arrest, mentioned in Mark's Gospel, was Mark himself: "And a certain young man followed Him, having a linen cloth cast around his naked body. And the young men took hold of him, and he left the linen cloth and fled from them naked" (14:51–52).

SO WHAT?

Suffering and loss aren't necessarily bad things—in fact, for Christians, they're the pathway to real life (8:35).

DAY 294

MARK 1–3

John the Baptist prepares the way for Jesus. The Lord calls disciples, heals the sick, and says whoever does God's will is "My brother and My sister and mother."

DAY 295

MARK 4–6

Jesus teaches in parables, drives many demons from a man called Legion, raises a nobleman's daughter from the dead, and walks on the stormy Sea of Galilee.

DAY 296

MARK 7–9

Jesus criticizes the hypocritical Pharisees, blesses a non-Jewish woman, performs miracles, and is transfigured. Peter recognizes Jesus as the Christ, or Messiah, the Jews are expecting.

DAY 297

MARK 10–11

Jesus rides into Jerusalem on a donkey, fulfilling a prophecy of Zechariah. The chief priests and scribes and elders of Israel question His authority.

DAY 298

MARK 12–13

Jesus says the greatest commandment in the law is "love the Lord your God with all your heart and with all your soul and with all your mind and with all your strength."

DAY 299

MARK 14–16

Jesus is arrested, and Peter fearfully denies knowing Him. Jesus dies on a cross, is buried, and rises again. He tells His disciples, "Go into all the world and preach the gospel."

LUKE

AUTHOR

Not stated but traditionally attributed to Luke, a Gentile physician (Colossians 4:14) and a missionary companion of the apostle Paul (2 Timothy 4:11).

DATE

Possibly the AD 70s–80s, as the gospel was spreading throughout the Roman Empire.

IN TEN WORDS OR LESS

Jesus is Savior of all people, whether Jew or Gentile.

DETAILS, PLEASE

Luke's Gospel is addressed to a man named Theophilus (1:3), "to set in order a declaration of those things that are most surely believed among us" about Jesus Christ (1:1). It's unclear who Theophilus was, though some believe he may have been a Roman official—and Luke's book is the least Jewish and most universal of the four Gospels. Luke traces Jesus' genealogy beyond Abraham, the patriarch of the Jews, all the way back to Adam, "the son of God" (3:38), common ancestor of everyone. Luke also shows Jesus' compassion for all people: Roman soldiers (7:1–10), widows (7:11–17), the "sinful" (7:36–50), the chronically ill (8:43–48), lepers (17:11–19), and many others—including a criminal condemned to die on a cross beside Jesus (23:40–43). As with all the Gospels, Luke shows Jesus' resurrection, adding detailed accounts of His appearances to two believers on the Emmaus road and the remaining eleven disciples. As the Gospel ends, Jesus is ascending into heaven—setting the stage for a sequel of sorts, Luke's book of Acts.

QUOTABLE

- "For where your treasure is, there your heart will be also." (12:34)

- "I say to you that likewise there shall be more joy in heaven over one sinner who repents than over ninety-nine righteous people who need no repentance." (15:7)
- "Whoever seeks to save his life shall lose it, and whoever loses his life shall preserve it." (17:33)
- "Whoever shall not receive the kingdom of God like a little child shall in no way enter it." (18:17)
- "For the Son of Man has come to seek and to save what was lost." (19:10)

UNIQUE AND UNUSUAL

Luke is the only Gospel to share Jesus' stories ("parables") of the good Samaritan (10:25–37), the prodigal son (15:11–32), and the rich man and Lazarus (16:19–31). Luke is also the only Gospel to detail Jesus' actual birth and words He spoke in childhood (both in chapter 2).

SO WHAT?

It doesn't matter who you are, where you come from, or what you've done—Jesus came to seek and to save you.

DAY 300

LUKE 1

Luke gathers eyewitness accounts of the life and ministry of Jesus. Luke begins with Jesus' miraculous conception and the birth of His relative John the Baptist.

DAY 301

LUKE 2–3

Jesus is born to the virgin Mary in Bethlehem, then dedicated at the temple. Years later, at about age thirty, He is baptized by John and begins His public ministry.

DAY 302

LUKE 4–5

Jesus defeats Satan's temptations in the wilderness. Then, in the Nazareth synagogue, He says He is the fulfillment of Isaiah's Messianic prophecy.

DAY 303

LUKE 6–7

Luke records a shortened version of Jesus' Sermon on the Mount and describes His healing of a Roman centurion's servant.

DAY 304

LUKE 8–9

Jesus preaches and heals throughout Galilee, then stills a storm on the sea. He sends His twelve disciples out to preach and is transfigured in front of Peter, James, and John.

DAY 305

LUKE 10–11

Jesus sends seventy other followers out to preach. He speaks the parable of the good Samaritan and mentions "the sign of Jonah"—the three days He will spend in the grave.

DAY 306

LUKE 12–13

Jesus warns of the Pharisees' hypocritical ways. He tells people that He will divide family members, and He calls everyone to repent.

DAY 307

LUKE 14–15

Jesus heals a diseased man on the sabbath, then tells the grumbling Pharisees the parable of the lost son—God welcomes the humble, any who "was lost and is found."

DAY 308

LUKE 16–17

Jesus' story of the rich man and Lazarus warns of hell. Jesus commands forgiveness to anyone who asks, and He tells of His second coming.

DAY 309

LUKE 18–19

Jesus blesses little children and heals a blind man. Jesus welcomes the tax collector Zacchaeus into God's kingdom, then makes His "triumphal entry" into Jerusalem.

DAY 310

LUKE 20:1–22:38

Jesus answers the Pharisees' trick question on taxes by saying, "Render to Caesar the things that are Caesar's, and to God the things that are God's."

DAY 311

LUKE 22:39–24:53

Jesus is betrayed and mocked. On the cross, He welcomes a repentant thief into God's kingdom. After His resurrection, He meets several times with His disciples, to help them "understand the scriptures."

KNOW YOUR BIBLE *MEN*

JOHN THE BAPTIST

HUMBLE AND WILD

And the same John had his clothing of camel's hair and a leather belt around his loins, and his food was locusts and wild honey.
MATTHEW 3:4

†

There's the life you could live and the life you choose to live. The choice between the two is not always right versus wrong. Sometimes, it's a choice between good and better.

Jesus' relative John could have been a priest like his father. He could have lived an easy life, serving in the comforts of the city. Instead, John chose to live off the land. He became an itinerant preacher, traveling around Israel and speaking to crowds about the coming Messiah. He baptized people as a sign of their repentance from sin and earned himself the nickname "the Baptist." Jesus said there was no man greater than John (Matthew 11:11).

John's life was short. It was ended by a government official who probably felt convicted and foolish when John boldly called him out for adultery (Matthew 14:1–12). The picture we're given of John is that he was wildly committed to Jesus. He was so awed by his Savior that he didn't even feel worthy to carry Jesus' sandals (Matthew 3:11). Yet God used this humble, wild man to prepare others to meet Jesus. He used John's boldness to drive away corruption and encourage repentance (Matthew 3:5–10).

John the Baptist may not have lived as comfortably as he could have as a priest, but he chose to give his life to Jesus. What will you choose to do with yours?

Dear God, I thank You for John's story. How can I serve You with my life? How can I point others to Jesus? Please help me to make good choices along the way. Help me to follow Your path.

JOHN

AUTHOR

Not stated but traditionally attributed to John, the "disciple whom Jesus loved" (John 21:7), brother of James and son of Zebedee (Matthew 4:21).

DATE

Around the AD 90s, as the last Gospel written.

IN TEN WORDS OR LESS

Jesus is God Himself, the only Savior of the world.

DETAILS, PLEASE

While the books of Matthew, Mark, and Luke have many similarities (they're called the "synoptic Gospels," meaning they take a common view), the book of John stands alone. The fourth Gospel downplays Jesus' parables (none are recorded) and miracles (only seven are featured). Instead, John provides more extensive treatments of Jesus' reasons for coming to earth ("I have come that they might have life, and that they might have it more abundantly," 10:10); His intimate relationship with God the Father ("My Father and I are one," 10:30); and His own feelings toward the job He had come to do ("Father, the hour has come. Glorify Your Son, that Your Son may also glorify You, as You have given Him power over all flesh, that He should give eternal life to as many as You have given Him," 17:1–2). John also gives special emphasis to Jesus' patient treatment of the disciples Thomas, who doubted the resurrection (20:24–29), and Peter, who had denied the Lord (21:15–23).

QUOTABLE

- In the beginning was the Word, and the Word was with God, and the Word was God. (1:1)
- "For God so loved the world that He gave His only begotten Son, that whoever believes in Him should not perish but have everlasting life." (3:16)

- "I am the bread of life." (6:35)
- "I am the good shepherd. The good shepherd gives His life for the sheep." (10:11)
- "I am the way, the truth, and the life. No man comes to the Father except through Me." (14:6)

UNIQUE AND UNUSUAL

Jesus' very first miracle, His changing of water into wine at a wedding in Cana, is recorded only in John's Gospel (2:1–12). So is His raising of Lazarus from the dead (11:1–44), His healing of a man born blind (9:1–38), and His long-distance healing of a nobleman's son (4:46–54). John is also the only Gospel to mention Nicodemus, who heard Jesus' teaching, "You must be born again" (3:7).

SO WHAT?

"These are written that you might believe that Jesus is the Christ, the Son of God, and that believing you might have life through His name" (20:31).

DAY 312

JOHN 1–3

Jesus is "the Word," who is God, and through whom the world was made. He promises that whoever believes in Him "should not perish but have everlasting life."

DAY 313

JOHN 4–5

Jesus tells a Samaritan woman that He is the Messiah; He tells the Jewish leaders, "I seek not My own will but the will of the Father who has sent Me."

DAY 314

JOHN 6–7

Jesus feeds five thousand people with a boy's lunch and calls Himself "the living bread that came down from heaven." Peter calls Jesus "the Christ, the Son of the living God."

DAY 315

JOHN 8–9

Jesus protects a woman caught in sin and calls Himself "the light of the world." He heals a man born blind, setting off more trouble with the Pharisees.

DAY 316

JOHN 10–11

Jesus describes Himself as the good shepherd who "gives His life for the sheep." He claims to be God: "My Father and I are one." Jesus raises Lazarus from the dead.

DAY 317

JOHN 12–13

People cheer Jesus as king in His triumphal entry into Jerusalem. He eats His last supper with the disciples and tells of His coming betrayal by Judas Iscariot.

DAY 318

JOHN 14–16

Jesus warns His followers that they will face persecution. But He promises that He will "prepare a place" for them and send them "another Comforter," the Holy Spirit, after His resurrection.

DAY 319

JOHN 17–18

Jesus prays for His disciples, and for all who will believe in Him through their preaching. He is arrested, denied by Peter, and tried before the Roman governor Pilate.

DAY 320

JOHN 19–21

Jesus dies on a cross, saying, "It is finished." Three days later, He returns to life. Jesus forgives Peter's denial, telling him, "Feed My sheep."

ACTS

AUTHOR

Not stated but traditionally attributed to Luke, a Gentile physician (Colossians 4:14), a missionary companion of the apostle Paul (2 Timothy 4:11), and the author of the Gospel of Luke.

DATE

Covering events of the AD 30s–60s, Acts was probably written sometime between AD 62 and 80.

IN TEN WORDS OR LESS

The Holy Spirit's arrival heralds the beginning of the Christian church.

DETAILS, PLEASE

Officially called "Acts of the Apostles," the book of Acts is a bridge between the story of Jesus in the Gospels and the life of the church in the letters that follow. Luke begins with Jesus' ascension into heaven after forty days of post-resurrection activity, "speaking of the things pertaining to the kingdom of God" (1:3). Ten days later, God sends the Holy Spirit on the festival day of Pentecost—and the church is born. Through the Spirit, the disciples are empowered to preach boldly about Jesus, and three thousand people become Christians that day. Jewish leaders, fearing the new movement called "this Way" (9:2), begin persecuting believers, who scatter to other areas and spread the gospel through much of the known world. The ultimate persecutor, Saul, becomes a Christian himself after meeting the brightly shining, heavenly Jesus on the road to Damascus. Saul, later called Paul, ultimately joins Peter and other Christian leaders in preaching, working miracles, and strengthening the fledgling church.

QUOTABLE

- "Men of Galilee, why do you stand gazing up into heaven? This same Jesus, who has been taken up from you to heaven, shall so come in similar manner as you have seen Him go into heaven." (1:11)

- "Repent, and every one of you be baptized in the name of Jesus Christ for the remission of sins, and you shall receive the gift of the Holy Spirit." (2:38)
- "Nor is there salvation in any other, for there is no other name under heaven given among men by which we must be saved." (4:12)
- "Saul, Saul, why are you persecuting Me?" (9:4)

UNIQUE AND UNUSUAL

Acts tells of the first Christian martyr, Stephen, stoned to death for blaming Jewish leaders for the death of Jesus (chapter 7). Acts also depicts the gospel's transition from a purely Jewish message to one for all people (9:15; 10:45) and the beginning of the Christian missionary movement (chapter 13).

SO WHAT?

Christians today are driven by the same force that Acts describes: "You shall receive power after the Holy Spirit has come on you" (1:8).

DAY 321

ACTS 1–2

Forty days after His resurrection, Jesus ascends into heaven. On the holiday called Pentecost, the Holy Spirit comes to believers. Peter preaches in Jerusalem, and three thousand are saved.

DAY 322

ACTS 3–5

Peter and John heal a lame man in Jesus' name, bringing persecution on the believers. A couple in the early church dies after presenting an offering dishonestly.

DAY 323

ACTS 6–7

Deacons are chosen to help with the care of the early church. One of them, Stephen, is martyred for his strong preaching to the Jewish leaders.

DAY 324

ACTS 8–9

The church is persecuted and scattered. A leader of the persecution, Saul, is saved after Jesus blinds him on the road to Damascus. Barnabas, a faithful Christian, convinces other believers to accept their former enemy.

DAY 325

ACTS 10–12

God welcomes Gentiles to salvation by having Peter share the gospel with the centurion Cornelius. Christians running from persecution take the message to other areas.

DAY 326

ACTS 13–14

In the city of Antioch, where believers were first called "Christians," God selects Saul and Barnabas for missionary service. Saul becomes known as Paul.

DAY 327

ACTS 15–17

Jesus' apostles announce that Christians do not need to follow Jewish traditions like circumcision. Paul begins a second missionary journey, through Asia Minor and Greece.

DAY 328

ACTS 18–19

Paul spends a year and a half in Corinth, facing Jewish opposition. In Ephesus, silversmiths riot over his message, which hurts their idol-making business.

DAY 329

ACTS 20–22

Paul returns to Jerusalem, where his opponents stir up a riot. Roman soldiers step in, allowing Paul to defend himself before the crowd. The people call for Paul's death.

DAY 330

ACTS 23–25

In connection with the riot, Paul faces the Sanhedrin (the Jewish ruling council) and then the Roman leaders Felix and Festus. As a Roman citizen, he appeals his case to Caesar.

DAY 331

ACTS 26–28

Paul testifies to King Agrippa and is sent to Rome. On his way to Rome, Paul survives shipwreck and a poisonous snake bite on the shore of Malta. Acts ends with Paul in Rome, preaching and teaching from a rented house.

ROMANS

AUTHOR

The apostle Paul (1:1), with the secretarial assistance of Tertius (16:22).

DATE

Approximately AD 57, near the conclusion of Paul's third missionary journey.

IN TEN WORDS OR LESS

Sinners are saved only by faith in Jesus Christ.

DETAILS, PLEASE

Some call Romans a "theology textbook" for its thorough explanation of the Christian life. Paul begins by describing God's righteous anger against human sin (chapters 1–2), noting that everyone falls short of God's standard (3:23). But God Himself provides the only way to overcome that sin, "the righteousness of God that is by faith in Jesus Christ, to all and on all those who believe" (3:22). Being justified (made right) through faith in Jesus, we can consider ourselves "to be dead indeed to sin but alive to God through Jesus Christ our Lord" (6:11). God's Spirit will "revive" (8:11) all who believe in Jesus, allowing us to "present [our] bodies as a living sacrifice, holy, acceptable to God" (12:1). It is possible, with God's help, to "not be overcome by evil, but [to] overcome evil with good" (12:21).

QUOTABLE

- All have sinned and come short of the glory of God. (3:23)
- God demonstrates His love toward us, in that while we were still sinners, Christ died for us. (5:8)
- The wages of sin is death, but the gift of God is eternal life through Jesus Christ our Lord. (6:23)

- Wretched man that I am! Who shall deliver me from the body of this death? I thank God through Jesus Christ our Lord. (7:24–25)
- We know that all things work together for good to those who love God, to those who are the called according to His purpose. (8:28)
- Owe no man anything but to love one another, for he who loves another has fulfilled the law. (13:8)
- Love works no ill to his neighbour; therefore love is the fulfilling of the law. (13:10)

UNIQUE AND UNUSUAL

Unlike Paul's other letters to churches, Romans was addressed to a congregation he'd never met. The great missionary was hoping to see the Roman Christians personally while traveling westward to Spain (15:23–24). It's unclear if Paul ever actually reached Spain or if he was executed in Rome after the end of the book of Acts.

SO WHAT?

In Paul's own words, "Therefore, being justified by faith, we have peace with God through our Lord Jesus Christ" (5:1).

DAY 332

ROMANS 1–3

To believers in Rome, Paul explains humanity's guilt before God. The sin problem can only be corrected by faith in Jesus Christ.

DAY 333

ROMANS 4–7

Justification is by faith and leads to "peace with God through our Lord Jesus Christ." Believers must think of themselves as dead to sin but alive to God through Jesus.

DAY 334

ROMANS 8–10

For those who are "in Christ Jesus," there is no condemnation for sin. Nothing—troubles, stress, persecution, famine, or sword—can separate us from His love.

DAY 335

ROMANS 11–13

Christians should offer themselves to God as "a living sacrifice," renewing their minds and not being "conformed to this world."

DAY 336

ROMANS 14–16

Christians enjoy freedom from religious rules. But they should honor the beliefs of others, helping with "the frailties of the weak," and not seeking "to please ourselves."

KNOW YOUR BIBLE *MEN*

JESUS

THE REAL GOD

The Son is the image of the invisible God, the firstborn over all creation.
COLOSSIANS 1:15 NIV

†

The U.S. Department of Treasury estimates that millions of dollars of counterfeit bills are in circulation. The easiest way for officials to quickly find them isn't to study all these fakes. Instead, they study real money down to the tiniest detail—that makes it easy to see when something is off. The best way to spot a counterfeit is to truly known the real thing.

When Paul wrote to the Colossians, they were struggling with counterfeit Jesuses. Cults and false ideas about God were spreading rapidly. Rather than trying to dispel every false idea floating around the city, Paul reminded the believers of who Jesus is:

Jesus is God (Colossians 1:15, 19), Jesus is the creator of all things (1:16), Jesus is the ruler of creation (1:15, 17), Jesus is the head of the church (1:18), Jesus is the reconciler who restores our relationship with God (1:20, 22).

Unfortunately, there is evil in the world. You will hear counterfeit ideas about God your whole life. How can you avoid the lies? By getting to know the real Jesus. The Bible reveals His wisdom, goodness, power, and love. Spend time in prayer talking directly with Jesus (Philippians 4:6–7). Spend time studying His wisdom (Proverbs 3:5–6). Spend time putting His teachings into practice (Matthew 5:16). You won't be fooled by a fake when you know the real thing.

Lord Jesus, I believe God the Father sent You—and that you are God. You are wise, good, powerful, and loving. I trust You for the forgiveness of my sins. Please help me to live every day to serve You. Thank You for loving me so much.

1 CORINTHIANS

AUTHOR

The apostle Paul, with the assistance of Sosthenes (1:1).

DATE

Approximately AD 55–57.

IN TEN WORDS OR LESS

An apostle tackles sin problems in the church at Corinth.

DETAILS, PLEASE

Paul had helped found the church in Corinth (Acts 18) but then moved on to other mission fields. While in Ephesus, he learns of serious problems in the Corinthian congregation and writes a long letter to address those issues. For those arguing over who should lead the church, Paul urges "that you be perfectly joined together in the same mind and in the same judgment" (1:10). For a man involved in an immoral relationship with his stepmother, Paul commands, "Put away that wicked person from among yourselves" (5:13). For those church members filing lawsuits against others, Paul warns, "Do you not know that the unrighteous shall not inherit the kingdom of God?" (6:9). The apostle also teaches on marriage, Christian liberty, the Lord's Supper, spiritual gifts, and the resurrection of the dead. In the famous thirteenth chapter of 1 Corinthians, Paul describes the "more excellent way" (12:31): that of charity, or love.

QUOTABLE

- For the preaching of the cross is foolishness to those who are perishing, but to us who are saved it is the power of God. (1:18)
- The foolishness of God is wiser than men, and the weakness of God is stronger than men. (1:25)
- For no man can lay a foundation other than what is laid, which is Jesus Christ. (3:11)

- Take heed lest this liberty of yours by any means becomes a stumbling block to those who are weak. (8:9)
- I have become all things to all men, that by all means I might save some. (9:22)
- For as often as you eat this bread and drink this cup, you declare the Lord's death until He comes. (11:26)
- Though I speak with the tongues of men and of angels, and have not love, I have become as sounding brass or a tinkling cymbal. (13:1)

UNIQUE AND UNUSUAL

Refuting opponents who questioned his apostleship, Paul insists that he is as much an apostle as Jesus' original disciples. "Am I not an apostle?" he asks in 1 Corinthians 9:1. "Have I not seen Jesus Christ our Lord?"

SO WHAT?

Church problems are nothing new—neither is the way to correct them. Personal purity, self-discipline, and love for others are vital to a congregation's success.

DAY 337

1 CORINTHIANS 1–6

The apostle Paul scolds Corinthian Christians for allowing a sinful relationship in their church, as well as for taking each other to court.

DAY 338

1 CORINTHIANS 7–10

Paul defends his leadership against people who criticize him. He warns them from Israel's history, and says, "whatever you do, do all for the glory of God."

DAY 339

1 CORINTHIANS 11–13

Paul describes the kinds of spiritual gifts that God gives Christians. He urges people to use their gifts to help "the body of Christ." Love must control every word and action.

DAY 340

1 CORINTHIANS 14–16

Jesus' resurrection is a sign that all who follow Him will be raised to eternal life. "This corruptible must put on incorruption, and this mortal must put on immortality."

2 CORINTHIANS

AUTHOR

The apostle Paul, with Timothy's assistance (1:1).

DATE

Approximately AD 55–57, shortly after the writing of 1 Corinthians.

IN TEN WORDS OR LESS

Paul defends his ministry to the troubled Corinthian church.

DETAILS, PLEASE

Corinthian believers had apparently addressed some of the problems Paul's first letter mentioned—though there were still troublemakers who questioned his authority. He was forced to speak "foolishly" (11:21), boasting of hardships he'd faced serving Jesus: "more abundant in labors, above measure in beatings, more frequent in prisons, often near death" (11:23). Paul even suffered a "thorn in the flesh" (12:7), which God refused to take away, telling him instead, "My grace is sufficient for you, for My strength is made perfect in weakness" (12:9). His parting warning: "Examine yourselves to see whether you are in the faith. Prove your own selves" (13:5).

QUOTABLE

- For He has made Him who knew no sin to be sin for us, that we might be made the righteousness of God in Him. (5:21)

UNIQUE AND UNUSUAL

Paul never identifies his "thorn in the flesh," though some speculate it may have been bad eyesight, temptations, even physical unattractiveness.

SO WHAT?

Christians should respect authority—whether in the church, the home, or society at large.

DAY 341

2 CORINTHIANS 1–5

The gospel ministry can be very difficult. But Paul says, "we have this treasure in earthen vessels, that the excellency of the power may be from God and not from us."

DAY 342

2 CORINTHIANS 6–9

Paul urges the Corinthians to give toward an offering for persecuted believers in Jerusalem. He tells them to give "bountifully," noting, "God loves a cheerful giver."

DAY 343

2 CORINTHIANS 10–13

Paul warns the Corinthians against false teachers. He reminds the church of his sufferings on their behalf and describes a vision of heaven that God gave him.

GALATIANS

AUTHOR

The apostle Paul (1:1).

DATE

Perhaps around AD 49, as one of Paul's earliest letters.

IN TEN WORDS OR LESS

Christians are free from restrictive Jewish laws.

DETAILS, PLEASE

Writing to several regional churches, Paul can only "marvel" (1:6) that Galatian Christians have turned from their freedom in Jesus back to the rules of Old Testament Judaism. Some people tried to compel Christians "to live as the Jews do" (2:14), an error even the apostle Peter made (2:11–13). Paul argued strongly "that no man is justified by the law in the sight of God. . .for, 'the just shall live by faith'" (3:11).

QUOTABLE

- But though we or an angel from heaven preach any other gospel to you than what we have preached to you, let him be accursed. (1:8)
- "I am crucified with Christ; nevertheless, I live, yet not I, but Christ lives in me, and the life that I now live in the flesh I live by the faith of the Son of God, who loved me and gave Himself for me." (2:20)
- O foolish Galatians, who has bewitched you that you should not obey the truth, before whose eyes Jesus Christ has been evidently set forth, crucified among you? (3:1)
- The fruit of the Spirit is love, joy, peace, long-suffering, gentleness, goodness, faith, meekness, self-control. Against such there is no law. (5:22–23)

UNIQUE AND UNUSUAL

One of Paul's closing comments, "You see how large a letter I have written to you with my own hand" (6:11), makes some believe that poor eyesight was the apostle's "thorn in the flesh" (2 Corinthians 12:7).

SO WHAT?

Old Testament rules don't control Christians' lives—but God's Spirit should: "Walk in the Spirit, and you shall not fulfill the lust of the flesh" (5:16).

DAY 344

GALATIANS 1–6

People are made right with God by faith in Jesus Christ, not by their good works. The spiritual life results in "fruit" such as love, joy, peace, long-suffering, and gentleness.

EPHESIANS

AUTHOR

The apostle Paul (1:1).

DATE

Around AD 62, toward the end of Paul's life.

IN TEN WORDS OR LESS

Christians are all members of Jesus' "body," the church.

DETAILS, PLEASE

Paul had started the church in Ephesus (Acts 19) and now explains in detail the church members' relationship to Jesus Christ—so that they "may grow up in all things into Him who is the head, even Christ" (4:15). Through Jesus, God has reconciled both Jews and Gentiles to Himself (2:11–18). This new life should result in pure, honest living in the church and in the home (chapters 4–6).

QUOTABLE

- Blessed be the God and Father of our Lord Jesus Christ, who has blessed us with all spiritual blessings in the heavenly places in Christ. (1:3)
- Therefore I also, after I heard of your faith in the Lord Jesus and love for all the saints, do not cease to give thanks for you, making mention of you in my prayers. (1:15–16)
- By grace you are saved through faith, and that not of yourselves; it is the gift of God, not of works, lest any man should boast. (2:8–9)
- To me, who am less than the least of all saints, is this grace given, that I should preach among the Gentiles the unsearchable riches of Christ. (3:8)

- Put on the whole armor of God, that you may be able to stand against the schemes of the devil. (6:11)

UNIQUE AND UNUSUAL

Paul tells servants (slaves, in today's language) to "be obedient to those who are your masters" (6:5). Why? Because God will reward such behavior (6:8).

SO WHAT?

"In [Jesus] you also are built together for a dwelling of God through the Spirit" (2:22).

DAY 345

EPHESIANS 1–6

In Jesus Christ, Jews and Gentiles become one. Putting on "the new man," believers "walk in love" and wear the "whole armor of God" to stand against Satan's attacks.

KNOW YOUR BIBLE *MEN*

AN UNNAMED MAN

STRUGGLING TO BELIEVE

Immediately the boy's father exclaimed,
"I do believe; help me overcome my unbelief!"
MARK 9:24 NIV

†

Do you ever struggle to believe in God? Unbelief is something most guys won't talk about in church. But there's so much heavy-duty stuff. . .Miracles are real? Jesus is God? He died for my sins? Sometimes, it can be hard to take in everything the Bible says.

An unnamed man in the book of Mark says the very thing that we may struggle to say: Help me believe. A demon has afflicted the man's son for years. So dad brings the boy to Jesus and asks for help. Jesus says, "Everything is possible for one who believes" (Mark 9:23 NIV). "I do believe," the man shouts desperately. "Help me overcome my unbelief!" What's amazing is how Jesus reacts. He doesn't criticize or punish the man. Instead, he frees the boy and sends the family joyfully on their way.

Struggling to believe is part of growing into a mature follower of Christ. It's similar to the way muscles tear when you lift weights—your muscles can't grow without some amount of torn tissue. In your spiritual muscle building, know that God is ready and willing to help. If you struggle to believe anything about the Christian faith, talk about it with God in prayer. Don't try to pretend you have a handle on things you truly struggle with. Let God hear your struggles and help to grow your faith.

Heavenly Father, please help my unbelief. Please strengthen me when I'm struggling. Reassure me with Your Spirit and show me the next step to take. I thank You for loving and guiding me each day.

PHILIPPIANS

AUTHOR

The apostle Paul, along with Timothy (1:1).

DATE

Probably the early 60s AD.

IN TEN WORDS OR LESS

"Friendship letter" between the apostle Paul and a beloved church.

DETAILS, PLEASE

With sixteen references to "joy" and "rejoicing," Philippians is one of the apostle Paul's most upbeat letters—even though he wrote it in "chains" (1:13). Paul thanks the church at Philippi for its support (1:5) and encourages its people to "rejoice in the Lord always, and again I say, rejoice" (4:4).

QUOTABLE

- For God is my witness, how greatly I long after you all in the heart of Jesus Christ. (1:8)
- For to me to live is Christ, and to die is gain. (1:21)
- Only let your conduct be as is proper for the gospel of Christ, that whether I come and see you or else be absent, I may hear of your affairs, that you stand fast in one spirit, with one mind striving together for the faith of the gospel. (1:27)
- I press toward the mark for the prize of the high calling of God in Christ Jesus. (3:14)
- Be anxious for nothing, but in everything, by prayer and supplication with thanksgiving, let your requests be made known to God. (4:6)

UNIQUE AND UNUSUAL

Though unity is a common theme in Paul's letters, he singles out two Philippian women, Euodia and Syntyche, pleading that they "be of the same mind in the Lord" (4:2).

SO WHAT?

When we live in the joy of the Lord, "the peace of God, which passes all understanding, shall guard your hearts and minds through Christ Jesus" (4:7).

DAY 346

PHILIPPIANS 1–4

Christians should always "rejoice in the Lord," trading worry for "prayer and supplication with thanksgiving." Then God will send His peace.

COLOSSIANS

AUTHOR

The apostle Paul, along with Timothy (1:1).

DATE

Probably the early 60s AD.

IN TEN WORDS OR LESS

Jesus Christ is supreme—over everyone and everything.

DETAILS, PLEASE

False teaching ("enticing words," 2:4) had infiltrated the church at Colosse, apparently causing some people to add unnecessary and unhelpful elements to their Christian faith. Paul sent this letter to remind Christians of the superiority of Jesus over Jewish rules and regulations (2:16), angels (2:18), and anything else. Jesus is "the image of the invisible God, the firstborn of every creature" (1:15).

QUOTABLE

- For this reason we also, since the day we heard it, do not cease to pray for you. (1:9)
- As you have therefore received Christ Jesus the Lord, so walk in Him, rooted and built up in Him, and established in the faith, as you have been taught, abounding in it with thanksgiving. (2:6–7)
- Set your affection on things above, not on things on the earth. (3:2)
- Let the peace of God rule in your hearts, to which you also are called in one body. And be thankful. (3:15)

- And whatever you do, do it heartily, as to the Lord, and not to men, knowing that from the Lord you shall receive the reward of the inheritance, for you serve the Lord Christ. (3:23–24)

UNIQUE AND UNUSUAL

Paul mentions a letter to Laodicea (4:16) that apparently did not make the cut as New Testament scripture.

SO WHAT?

"Beware lest any man seduce you through philosophy and vain deceit, according to the tradition of men. . .and not according to Christ" (2:8).

DAY 347

COLOSSIANS 1–4

Jesus is "the image of the invisible God." In Him "dwells all the fullness of the Godhead bodily." Raised with Jesus, believers should set their minds on heavenly things.

1 THESSALONIANS

AUTHOR

The apostle Paul, along with Silvanus (Silas) and Timothy (1:1).

DATE

The early 50s AD—perhaps Paul's earliest letter.

IN TEN WORDS OR LESS

Jesus will return to gather His followers to Him.

DETAILS, PLEASE

In this letter to another church he helped found (see Acts 17), Paul teaches on the second coming of Christ, apparently an issue of some concern to the Thessalonians. Paul describes how Jesus will return but doesn't say exactly when. The important thing, in his words, is "that you would walk worthy of God, who has called you to His kingdom and glory" (2:12).

QUOTABLE

- But we were gentle among you, even as a nurse cherishes her children. So, being affectionately desirous of you, we were willing to impart to you not only the gospel of God but also our own souls, because you were dear to us. (2:7–8)
- For this reason we also thank God without ceasing, because when you received the word of God that you heard from us, you received it not as the word of men but as it is in truth, the word of God, which also effectively works in you who believe. (2:13)
- For the Lord Himself shall descend from heaven with a shout, with the voice of the archangel, and with the trumpet of God. And the dead in Christ shall rise first. (4:16)

- The day of the Lord will come like a thief in the night. (5:2)

UNIQUE AND UNUSUAL

First Thessalonians contains two of the Bible's shortest verses: "Rejoice always" (5:16) and "Pray without ceasing" (5:17).

SO WHAT?

The Thessalonians were told to live right in view of Jesus' coming return. With the passage of two thousand years, don't you think it's more important for us today?

DAY 348

1 THESSALONIANS 1–5; 2 THESSALONIANS 1–3

While awaiting Jesus' return, all Christians should control their bodies "in sanctification and honor." In time, Jesus will pay back those who persecute believers.

2 THESSALONIANS

AUTHOR

The apostle Paul, along with Silvanus (Silas) and Timothy (1:1).

DATE

The early 50s AD—perhaps Paul's second-oldest letter.

IN TEN WORDS OR LESS

Christians should work until Jesus returns.

DETAILS, PLEASE

Shortly after writing 1 Thessalonians, Paul dictates a follow-up. Apparently, a letter falsely claiming to be from Paul had left the Thessalonians "shaken in mind. . .troubled" (2:2) at the thought that Jesus had already returned. Paul assures them that the event is still future—and urges everyone to live positive and productive lives until the second coming. "If any will not work," Paul commands those who have dropped out in anticipation of Jesus' return, "he should not eat" (3:10).

QUOTABLE

- The Lord is faithful, who shall establish you and keep you from evil. (3:3)
- Brothers, do not be weary in doing good. (3:13)

UNIQUE AND UNUSUAL

The fact that Paul dictated this letter is clear from his comment "The greeting of Paul with my own hand. . .so I write" (3:17).

SO WHAT?

As with all of the Christian life, balance is key: We should always look forward to Jesus' return, but we should also be busy doing good while we're here on earth.

1 TIMOTHY

AUTHOR

The apostle Paul (1:1).

DATE

Approximately AD 63.

IN TEN WORDS OR LESS

Pastors are taught how to conduct their lives and churches.

DETAILS, PLEASE

The first of three "pastoral epistles," 1 Timothy contains the aging apostle Paul's insights for a new generation of church leaders. Timothy had often worked alongside Paul but was now pastoring in Ephesus (1:3). Paul warned him against legalism and false teaching (chapter 1), listed the qualifications for pastors and deacons (chapter 3), and described the behavior of a "good minister of Jesus Christ" (4:6) in the final three chapters.

QUOTABLE

- Christ Jesus came into the world to save sinners, of whom I am chief. (1:15)
- I exhort therefore, first of all, that supplications, prayers, intercessions, and giving of thanks be made for all men, for kings and for all who are in authority, that we may lead a quiet and peaceful life in all godliness and honesty. (2:1–2)
- This is a true saying: if a man desires the office of a bishop, he desires a good work. (3:1)
- Do not let any man despise your youth, but be an example to the believers in word, in conduct, in love, in spirit, in faith, in purity. (4:12)

UNIQUE AND UNUSUAL

First Timothy seems to command good pay for pastors: "Let the elders who rule well be counted worthy of double honour. . . . 'The laborer is worthy of his reward'" (5:17–18).

SO WHAT?

Though 1 Timothy is a letter to a pastor, Paul's teaching "that you may know how you ought to behave yourself in the house of God" (3:15) can speak to the rest of us too.

DAY 349

1 TIMOTHY 1–6

The apostle Paul tells young Timothy how to lead the church. "Take heed to yourself and to the doctrine. . .for in doing this you shall save both yourself and those who hear you."

PETER

HELP WHEN YOU'RE DROWNING

But when he saw the wind was boisterous, he was afraid. And beginning to sink, he cried, saying, "Lord, save me!"
MATTHEW 14:30

†

Most guys don't like asking for help. We'd rather figure things out on our own. Few of us want to admit we can't do something. . .especially if we're stuck in a mess we made for ourselves.

Peter was great at making messes. The Gospels include several stories that make Peter look impulsive, foolish, or sinful (Matthew 16:21–28; 17:1–11; 26:69–75; John 18:1–11). But in Matthew 14:22–33, Peter demonstrates a great way to approach God—he cries out for help! After taking his eyes off Jesus, Peter quickly sank into a literal raging sea. But before he went under, Peter had the good sense to pray really fast for help.

Water isn't a requirement for you to feel like you're drowning. These teenage years are some of the busiest years in your life. Homework. Sports. Robotics club. Marching band. An afterschool job. Volunteering at church. Going on dates. Helping a sick relative. Divorce in the family. Peer pressure. Dealing with the fallout of a bad decision. Sometimes, life crushes you with waves of busyness and stress. When that happens, it's easy to take your eyes off Jesus. But it's never too late to ask Him for help.

No matter what's drowning you—even if it's a mess of your own making—God will hear your cries. Cry out and let Him pull you up from the raging sea.

Dear God, please help me with these things that are stressing me out right now. Please pull me out of this storm. I thank You for watching over me.

2 TIMOTHY

AUTHOR

The apostle Paul (1:1).

DATE

Probably the mid-60s AD.

IN TEN WORDS OR LESS

The apostle Paul's final words to a beloved coworker.

DETAILS, PLEASE

Second Timothy may be the last known letter of Paul. Addressed to "Timothy, my dearly beloved son" (1:2), the book warns the young pastor against false teaching and urges him to live a life of purity before his congregation. Timothy should expect trouble ("All who will live godly in Christ Jesus shall suffer persecution," 3:12), but God will be faithful ("The Lord shall deliver me from every evil work and will preserve me for His heavenly kingdom," 4:18). Paul begs Timothy to join him as quickly as possible, as "the time of my departure is at hand" (4:6).

QUOTABLE

- I am reminded of the sincere faith that is in you, which dwelled first in your grandmother Lois and your mother, Eunice, and I am persuaded that it is also in you. (1:5)
- Hold fast the form of sound words that you have heard from me, in faith and love that is in Christ Jesus. (1:13)
- You therefore endure hardship as a good soldier of Jesus Christ. (2:3)
- And the servant of the Lord must not quarrel but be gentle to all men, able to teach, patient, in meekness instructing those who oppose themselves, if God perhaps will give them repentance to the acknowledging of the truth. (2:24–25)

UNIQUE AND UNUSUAL

Paul tells where the Bible comes from in 2 Timothy: "All scripture is given by inspiration of God" (3:16). The idea of the word inspiration is "breathed out."

SO WHAT?

We should all live life in such a way that we can say, like Paul, "I have fought a good fight, I have finished my course, I have kept the faith" (4:7).

DAY 350

2 TIMOTHY 1–4; TITUS 1–3

Two more "pastoral letters" share Paul's instructions on church leadership. Timothy is to "endure hardship as a good soldier of Jesus." Titus is to "speak and exhort and rebuke with all authority."

TITUS

AUTHOR

The apostle Paul (1:1).

DATE

Approximately AD 63.

IN TEN WORDS OR LESS

Church leaders are instructed on their lives and teaching.

DETAILS, PLEASE

On the Mediterranean island of Crete, Paul left Titus to "set in order the things that are lacking and ordain elders" (1:5) for the fledgling church. Known for their poor behavior (see "Unique and Unusual" below), the people of Crete needed the kind of church leader who holds fast to "the faithful word as he has been taught, that he may be able, by sound doctrine, both to exhort and to convince those who contradict" (1:9).

QUOTABLE

- Not by works of righteousness that we have done, but according to His mercy He saved us, by the washing of regeneration and renewing of the Holy Spirit. (3:5)

UNIQUE AND UNUSUAL

Paul quotes a Cretan philosopher in this letter: "One of them, even a prophet of their own, said, 'The Cretans are always liars, evil beasts, lazy gluttons'" (1:12). The quotation is from Epimenides, of the sixth century BC.

SO WHAT?

Though church leaders are held to a high standard, so are the people in the pews. What's good for the pastor is good for everyone else.

PHILEMON

AUTHOR

The apostle Paul (verse 1).

DATE

Probably around AD 63, when Paul was imprisoned in Rome.

IN TEN WORDS OR LESS

Paul begs mercy for a runaway slave converted to Christianity.

DETAILS, PLEASE

Philemon is a "fellow laborer" (verse 1) of Paul, a man who has "refreshed" (verse 7) other Christians with his love and generosity. But the apostle writes with a deeper request—that Philemon forgive and take back a runaway slave, who apparently accepted Christ under Paul's teaching: "my son Onesimus, whom I have begotten in my imprisonment" (verse 10). "If you consider me therefore a partner," Paul wrote to Philemon, "receive him as myself" (verse 17).

QUOTABLE

- I thank my God, making mention of you always in my prayers, hearing of your love and faith, which you have toward the Lord Jesus and toward all saints. (verses 4–5)
- Having confidence in your obedience I wrote to you, knowing that you will also do more than I say. (verse 21)

UNIQUE AND UNUSUAL

With only one chapter and twenty-five verses, Philemon is the shortest of Paul's letters in the Bible.

SO WHAT?

Christians are called to forgive, and here's a practical example to consider. With God's help, will you let go of your grudges?

DAY 351

PHILEMON; HEBREWS 1–6

Philemon is urged to welcome back his runaway slave who became a Christian. Hebrews shows how Jesus and faith in Him are far better than the Old Testament rules.

DAY 352

HEBREWS 7–10

Old Testament law was just a "shadow of good things to come." Jesus, by shedding His perfect blood on the cross, "put away sin by the sacrifice of Himself."

DAY 353

HEBREWS 11–13

Old Testament heroes such as Noah, Abraham, and Moses obeyed God by faith, just as Christians do. We now "continually offer the sacrifice of praise to God."

HEBREWS

AUTHOR

Not stated; Paul, Luke, Barnabas, and Apollos have all been suggested.

DATE

Probably sometime before AD 70, since Hebrews refers to temple sacrifices. The Jerusalem temple was destroyed by Romans in AD 70.

IN TEN WORDS OR LESS

Jesus is better than any Old Testament person or sacrifice.

DETAILS, PLEASE

Written to Jewish Christians (hence the name "Hebrews"), this long letter emphasizes the superiority of Christianity to Old Testament Judaism. Jesus is "so much better" (1:4) than angels, Moses, and the previous animal sacrifices. "For if the blood of bulls and of goats and the ashes of a heifer sprinkling the unclean sanctifies to the purifying of the flesh," Hebrews asks, "how much more shall the blood of Christ, who through the eternal Spirit offered Himself without blemish to God, purge your conscience from dead works to serve the living God?" (9:13–14). Jewish Christians, some of whom were apparently wavering in their commitment to Jesus, are reminded that Christ "is also the mediator of a better covenant, which was established on better promises" (8:6)—a once-for-all sacrifice on the cross that provides "eternal redemption for us" (9:12).

QUOTABLE

- How shall we escape if we neglect so great a salvation? (2:3)
- Therefore there remains a rest for the people of God. (4:9)
- It is appointed for men to die once, but after this the judgment. (9:27)

- Not giving up the assembling of ourselves together, as is the manner of some, but exhorting one another, and so much the more as you see the Day approaching. (10:25)
- Now faith is the substance of things hoped for, the evidence of things not seen. (11:1)
- Therefore, since we also are surrounded by so great a cloud of witnesses, let us lay aside every weight, and the sin that so easily besets us, and let us run with patience the race that is set before us, looking to Jesus, the author and finisher of our faith. (12:1–2)
- Let brotherly love continue. (13:1)

UNIQUE AND UNUSUAL

Hebrews is one of only two New Testament letters (the other being 1 John) that includes no greeting or hint of its author.

SO WHAT?

"Therefore, brothers, having boldness to enter into the holiest by the blood of Jesus. . . , let us draw near with a true heart in full assurance of faith, having our hearts sprinkled from an evil conscience and our bodies washed with pure water" (10:19, 22).

JAMES

AUTHOR

James (1:1), probably a brother of Jesus (see Matthew 13:55; Mark 6:3).

DATE

Approximately AD 60.

IN TEN WORDS OR LESS

Real Christian faith is shown by one's good works.

DETAILS, PLEASE

Though the apostle Paul clearly taught that salvation is by faith alone and not by good works (see Romans 3:28), James clarifies that good works will follow true faith: "What does it profit, my brothers, though a man says he has faith and does not have works?" (2:14). James encourages Christians, in everyday life, to view trials as opportunities for spiritual growth, to control their tongues, to make peace, to avoid favoritism, and to help the needy. The bottom line? "Therefore to him who knows to do good and does not do it, to him it is sin" (4:17).

QUOTABLE

- Every good gift and every perfect gift is from above and comes down from the Father of lights, with whom there is no variation or shadow of turning. (1:17)
- But be doers of the word and not hearers only, deceiving your own selves. (1:22)
- Pure and undefiled religion before God and the Father is this: to visit the fatherless and widows in their affliction, and to keep himself unblemished from the world. (1:27)
- Draw near to God and He will draw near to you. (4:8)
- The effective fervent prayer of a righteous man avails much. (5:16)

UNIQUE AND UNUSUAL

For those who think it's enough just to believe in God, James says, "The demons also believe, and tremble" (2:19). Life-changing faith in Jesus is the key.

SO WHAT?

Want practical wisdom for living the Christian life? You'll find it all through the book of James.

DAY 354

JAMES 1–5

True Christian faith produces good works, such as caring for the poor. If we "draw near to God," He will draw near to us.

KNOW YOUR BIBLE *MEN*

PAUL

CHIEF OF SINNERS

This is a faithful saying and worthy of all acceptance, that Christ Jesus came into the world to save sinners, of whom I am chief.
1 TIMOTHY 1:15

†

Do you ever feel like you're too dirty for God to love? Like you're the worst person in the world? Sin makes us feel this way. Secrets. Partying. Porn. Deceiving your parents, teachers, or boss. Taking things too far on a date. These choices leave us feeling ashamed and unworthy of forgiveness. But you know what? You're not alone in the struggle. Every guy has some measure of sin in his life—even a guy who ended up writing much of the New Testament.

Saul was a smart and cunning Pharisee. Among the first-century Jews, Pharisees were powerful religious leaders. They harassed and sometimes killed people who threatened their way of life—including followers of Jesus (Acts 7:54–8:1). Saul hated Christians and used his power to hunt and imprison them (Acts 9:1–2). Yet God chose Saul—who would soon be known as Paul (Acts 13:9)—to be the premier Christian missionary. This murderous Pharisee who had committed terrible sins became God's messenger of the gospel of Christ. The Lord even inspired Paul to write several letters that became books in the New Testament—which we still read today!

Sin can make you feel like you're the worst person in the world, like you're too dirty for God to love. But that's a lie. God will never stop loving you, and He can purify you no matter what you've done (1 John 1:9). Your job is simply to confess your sins to God and, like Paul, allow Him to transform your life.

Dear God, please forgive me for my sins. I thank You for loving me. I thank You, Jesus, for paying the debt of my sins. Please transform my life into one that closely resembles Yours.

1 PETER

AUTHOR

The apostle Peter (1:1), with the assistance of Silas (5:12).

DATE

Approximately AD 65.

IN TEN WORDS OR LESS

Suffering for the sake of Jesus is noble and good.

DETAILS, PLEASE

As the early church grows, the Roman Empire begins persecuting Christians—and Peter assures them that God is still in control: "Beloved, do not think it strange concerning the fiery trial that is to test you as though some strange thing happened to you" (4:12). What is the proper response to such suffering? "Rejoice because you are partakers of Christ's sufferings, that when His glory shall be revealed, you may be glad also with exceeding joy" (4:13).

QUOTABLE

- Blessed be the God and Father of our Lord Jesus Christ, who according to His abundant mercy has begotten us again to a living hope through the resurrection of Jesus Christ from the dead, to an inheritance incorruptible and undefiled, and which does not fade away, reserved in heaven for you. (1:3–4)
- As newborn babies, desire the sincere milk of the word, that you may grow by it, if indeed you have tasted that the Lord is gracious. (2:2–3)
- Be sober, be vigilant, because your adversary the devil walks about like a roaring lion, seeking whom he may devour. (5:8)

UNIQUE AND UNUSUAL

Peter clarifies exactly how many people rode out the great flood on Noah's ark: eight (3:20). Genesis indicates that "Noah. . .and his sons, and his wife, and his sons' wives" (Genesis 7:7) were in the boat but leaves unsaid whether any sons might have had multiple wives.

SO WHAT?

Life may be hard, but God is always good. And for Christians, there's a much better day ahead.

DAY 355

1 PETER 1–5

Troubles are short term, but salvation lasts forever. With "the end of all things" nearing, Christians should live wisely and prayerfully.

2 PETER

AUTHOR

The apostle Peter (1:1).

DATE

Probably the late 60s AD, shortly before Peter's execution.

IN TEN WORDS OR LESS

Beware of false teachers within the church.

DETAILS, PLEASE

The Christian qualities of faith, virtue, knowledge, self-control, patience, godliness, and love (1:5–8), coupled with a reliance on scripture (1:19–21), will help believers avoid the false teachings of those who "shall secretly bring in destructive heresies, even denying the Lord who bought them" (2:1).

QUOTABLE

- We did not follow cunningly devised fables when we made known to you the power and coming of our Lord Jesus Christ, but were eyewitnesses of His majesty. (1:16)
- The Lord is not slow concerning His promise, as some men count slowness, but is long-suffering toward us, not willing that any should perish but that all should come to repentance. (3:9)
- But the day of the Lord will come like a thief in the night, in which the heavens shall pass away with a great noise, and the elements shall melt with fervent heat. The earth also and the works that are in it shall be burned up. (3:10)

UNIQUE AND UNUSUAL

Peter wrote this letter knowing his death was near: "Shortly I must put off this tent of mine, even as our Lord Jesus Christ has declared to me" (1:14).

SO WHAT?

"Beware lest you also fall from your own stedfastness, being led away with the error of the wicked" (3:17).

DAY 356

2 PETER 1–3

Beware of false teachers, who bring in "destructive heresies, even denying the Lord who bought them." Believers should grow in grace and their knowledge of Jesus.

1 JOHN

AUTHOR

Not stated but according to church tradition, the apostle John.

DATE

Approximately AD 92.

IN TEN WORDS OR LESS

Jesus was real man just as He is real God.

DETAILS, PLEASE

First John tackles a strange heresy that claimed Jesus had been on earth only in spirit, not in body: "Every spirit that does not confess that Jesus Christ has come in the flesh is not of God. And this is that spirit of antichrist" (4:3). John wrote that he knew Jesus personally, as one "which we have looked on and our hands have handled" (1:1), and that knowledge leads to a saving belief in Jesus. Saving belief leads to obedience, but even when we sin, we know that God "is faithful and just to forgive us our sins" when we confess (1:9).

QUOTABLE

- If we confess our sins, He is faithful and just to forgive us our sins and to cleanse us from all unrighteousness. (1:9)
- He who says he is in the light and hates his brother is in darkness even until now. (2:9)
- Behold, what manner of love the Father has bestowed on us, that we should be called the sons of God. (3:1)
- Beloved, let us love one another, for love is of God. . . . God is love. (4:7–8)

UNIQUE AND UNUSUAL

First John includes none of the usual features of a Bible letter—greetings, identification of the author, and the like. But it's a very warm, compassionate letter nonetheless.

SO WHAT?

"I have written these things. . .that you may know that you have eternal life" (5:13).

DAY 357

1 JOHN 1–5

Christians have been greatly loved by God and should therefore love each other. They are not to love "the things that are in the world."

2 JOHN

AUTHOR

The apostle John according to church tradition. The author is identified only as "the elder" (verse 1).

DATE

Approximately AD 92.

IN TEN WORDS OR LESS

Avoid false teachers who deny Jesus' physical life on earth.

DETAILS, PLEASE

Addressed to "the elect lady and her children" (verse 1), perhaps an actual family or, figuratively, a church, 2 John tackles the heretical idea that Jesus had not been physically present on earth. The letter may be a reaction to the "gnostics," who taught that Jesus was spirit only and that He just appeared to suffer and die on the cross. This teaching, of "a deceiver and an antichrist" (verse 7), should be avoided at all costs—to the point of barring one's door against those who believe it (verse 10).

QUOTABLE

- I rejoiced greatly that I found some of your children walking in truth, as we have received a commandment from the Father. (verse 4)
- I beseech you, lady, not as though I wrote a new commandment to you, but what we had from the beginning—that we love one another. (verse 5)
- This is love: that we walk according to His commandments. (verse 6)

UNIQUE AND UNUSUAL

Second John, one of the New Testament's four single-chapter books, is the shortest by verse count: thirteen.

SO WHAT?

Just as in John's time, false teachers spread dangerous ideas in today's world. Every teaching should be weighed against scripture, 2 John says. "He who abides in the doctrine of Christ has both the Father and the Son" (verse 9).

DAY 358

2 JOHN; 3 JOHN; JUDE

John urges Christians to reject false teachers. Jude calls believers to "contend for the faith that was once delivered to the saints."

KNOW YOUR BIBLE *MEN*

TIMOTHY

YOUNG INFLUENCER

Do not let any man despise your youth, but be an example to the believers in word, in conduct, in love, in spirit, in faith, in purity.
1 TIMOTHY 4:12

†

The internet is full of young influencers. They make cool videos, have large followings on social media, and get paid to test and review new products. This kind of influence isn't necessarily bad, but it's temporary. It only lasts until the next product comes out...or the next young influencer comes along.

Timothy was a young influencer with a long shelf life. He spent many years with the famous apostle Paul. Together, they traveled throughout the Roman Empire and started new churches. Eventually, it was time for Timothy to strike out on his own—and Paul wrote to Timothy a few words that ring true for us today: "Be an example to the believers in word, in conduct, in love, in spirit, in faith, in purity." That's real influence.

God wants to use you to influence others, but for more important reasons than selling the latest video game. He wants you to bring the good news of His love to others. What's the best way to do that? By setting an example. Jesus put it this way, "Let your light so shine before men, that they may see your good works and glorify your Father who is in heaven" (Matthew 5:16). Live in such a way that others are drawn to God. That is lasting influence.

Heavenly Father, help me to set an example of Your love and grace. I thank You for how You've changed my life. Please help me to live in such a way that others are drawn to glorify You.

3 JOHN

AUTHOR

The apostle John according to church tradition. The author is identified only as "the elder" (verse 1).

DATE

Approximately AD 92.

IN TEN WORDS OR LESS

Church leaders must be humble, not proud.

DETAILS, PLEASE

Addressed to a believer named Gaius, 3 John praises those (like Gaius and another Christian named Demetrius) who lead in "love before the church" (verse 6). But 3 John also has harsh words for Christians like Diotrephes, "who loves to have the preeminence" (verse 9) and refuse to show kindness and hospitality to traveling evangelists.

QUOTABLE

- Beloved, I wish above all things that you may prosper and be in health, even as your soul prospers. (verse 2)
- I have no greater joy than to hear that my children walk in truth. (verse 4)
- He who does good is of God, but he who does evil has not seen God. (verse 11)

UNIQUE AND UNUSUAL

Third John, one of four single-chapter books in the New Testament, is the second shortest by verse count: fourteen.

SO WHAT?

Hospitality isn't just for the party planners of the world—Christians are expected to feed, house, and encourage other believers, especially those who minister full-time for God. Humble service to others follows the example of Jesus Himself (see John 13:14).

JUDE

AUTHOR

Jude (verse 1), possibly Jesus' half brother (see Matthew 13:55; Mark 6:3).

DATE

Approximately AD 82.

IN TEN WORDS OR LESS

Beware of heretical teachers and their dangerous doctrines.

DETAILS, PLEASE

Jude tackles the same problems Peter did in his second letter: false teachers who were leading the early church astray. "Murmurers" and "complainers" who were "walking after their own lusts" (verse 16) were apparently using the grace of God as a cover for their sinful lifestyles—and encouraging Christian believers to do the same. True believers, Jude says, reflect God's love, show compassion, and work to pull sinners "out of the fire" (verse 23).

QUOTABLE

- You should earnestly contend for the faith that was once delivered to the saints. (verse 3)

UNIQUE AND UNUSUAL

Jude provides details of two Old Testament events not recorded in the Old Testament: the archangel Michael's fight with Satan over the body of Moses (verse 9) and Enoch's prophecy of God's judgment (verses 14–15).

SO WHAT?

Satan tries to sneak "secret agents" into God's church to confuse and ultimately crush true believers. It's the job of every true Christian to "earnestly contend for the faith" as passed down by Jesus' disciples and recorded in the Bible.

REVELATION

AUTHOR

John (1:1), probably the apostle.

DATE

Approximately AD 95.

IN TEN WORDS OR LESS

God will judge evil and reward His saints.

DETAILS, PLEASE

Jesus Christ Himself arranges for John to receive a "Revelation" of "things that must shortly come to pass" (1:1). First, in chapters 2–3, Jesus gives John words of challenge and/or encouragement for seven churches—the good, the bad, and the in-between. Then the vision turns to the actual throne room of God, where a Lamb, looking "as though it had been slain" (5:6), breaks seven seals from a scroll, unleashing war, famine, and other disasters on the earth. A dragon and two beasts, allied against God, arise to demand the worship of earth's people who have not been killed in the earlier catastrophes. The satanic forces and the people who follow them incur seven "vials of the wrath of God" (16:1), which bring plagues, darkness, and huge hailstones on earth. The upheaval destroys "Babylon the great," the evil and arrogant world system, just before an angel from heaven seizes Satan, "that old serpent" (20:2), and imprisons him for one thousand years. After a brief release to instigate a worldwide war, Satan is thrown into "the lake of fire and brimstone," where he will be "tormented day and night for ever and ever" (20:10). God unveils "a new heaven and a new earth" (21:1), where He will "wipe away all tears" (21:4) from His people's eyes.

QUOTABLE

- Blessed is he who reads and those who hear the words of this prophecy, and keep those things that are written in it. (1:3)
- "Worthy is the Lamb who was slain to receive power and riches and wisdom and strength and honor and glory and blessing." (5:12)

UNIQUE AND UNUSUAL

Revelation is an example of "apocalyptic literature," the only such book in the New Testament. Apocalyptic implies "revealing secret information." The book of Revelation identifies Jesus Christ as the "Alpha and Omega" (1:8) and reveals the number 666 as a sign of "the beast" (13:18).

SO WHAT?

"I've read the back of the book," an old Southern gospel song says, "and we win!" God has given His children a preview of how this world ends—and the new-and-improved world we'll enjoy forever. The curse of sin will be gone, we'll live in perfect fellowship with the Lord Himself, and we will "reign forever and ever" (22:5). Kind of puts our bad days in perspective, doesn't it?

DAY 359

REVELATION 1–3

Jesus gives John messages for seven churches of Asia Minor. They are urged to hold fast their faith, repent of their sins, or—as with the Ephesians—remember "your first love."

DAY 360

REVELATION 4–6

John sees into heaven's throne room, where a seven-sealed scroll is opened by Jesus, looking like "a Lamb as though it had been slain." Each seal pours God's anger on the earth.

DAY 361

REVELATION 7–10

When the final seal is broken, seven trumpets announce terrible "woes" on the earth. Despite the death and destruction, survivors "did not repent" of their idolatry and evil.

DAY 362

REVELATION 11–13

A dragon and two beasts rise up to oppose and insult God, leading people into false worship. Those who don't worship the second beast (identified by the number 666) are killed.

DAY 363

REVELATION 14–16

A "Lamb" appears on Mount Zion. An angel begins "the harvest of the earth." Seven vials of God's wrath are poured out. Armies gather for battle at a place called Armageddon.

DAY 364

REVELATION 17–19

"Babylon the Great," which rules over the kings of earth, is destroyed, and God's people are avenged. Jesus returns to earth to destroy the beast and his armies.

DAY 365

REVELATION 20–22

Satan is thrown into the lake of fire. God judges human beings, sending them either to eternal life or destruction. "The holy city, new Jerusalem" comes down from heaven to a restored earth.